CONTENTS

Unit 1	Hi!	2
Unit 2	Jobs	6
Self-Assessment Test 1 Units 1–2		11
Unit 3	Family life	12
Unit 4	Places	16
Self-Assessment Test 2 Units 3–4		21
Unit 5	Likes and dislikes	22
Unit 6	Routines	26
Self-Assessment Test 3 Units 5–6		31
Unit 7	Talent	32
Unit 8	Free time	36
Self-Assessment Test 4 Units 7–8		41
Unit 9	Changes	42
Unit 10	Travel	46
Self-Assessment Test 5 Units 9–10		51
Unit 11	Childhood	52
Unit 12	Shopping	56
Self-Assessment Test 6 Units 11–12		61
Self-Assessment Tests Answer Key		62
Workbook Tapescript		63

success

Beginner Workbook

Jennifer Parsons

PEARSON
Longman

01 Hi!

GRAMMAR AND SPEAKING

I'm/My name's/What's

1 Complete the conversations.

1 A Hello. <u>I'm</u> Karl. What's your name?
B <u>My</u> name's Dave.
A Nice to meet <u>you</u>, Dave.
B Nice to meet <u>you</u>, <u>too</u>!

2 A Hi. _____ Jim. What's your name?
B _____ name's Silvia.
A Nice to meet _____, Silvia.
B Nice to meet _____, _____!

3 A Hi. _____ Jane. What's _____ name?
B _____ name's Fernando.
A Nice to _____, Fernando.
B Nice to _____, _____!

4 A Hello. _____ Helen. What's _____?
B _____, Amélie.
A _____, _____.
B _____!

GRAMMAR AND VOCABULARY

Vocabulary: countries and nationalities

1 Complete countries 1–10.

1 M e x i c o
2 _ a _ a _ _
3 _ _ _ e _ _ i _ _
4 _ _ _ l _ n _
5 _ e _ _ a _ _
6 _ _ l _ _ d
7 _ r _ _ c _
8 _ _ a _ n
9 _ _ a _ _
10 _ u _ _ e _

2 **CD T2** Listen and write the country or nationality.

1 **Dave** I'm from _Canada_ .
  Amélie I'm _French_ .

2 **Silvia** I'm from _____ .
  Karl I'm _____ .

3 **Jane** I'm _____ .
  Fernando I'm _____ .

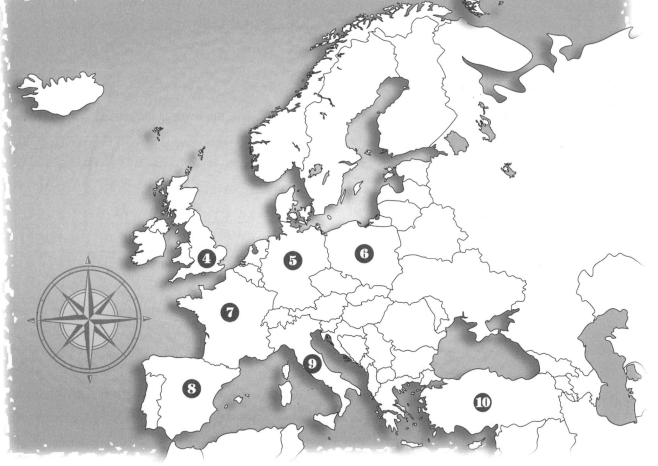

GRAMMAR AND SPEAKING

to be: am/are

1 Write the sentences.

1 Italy. / I / from / am
   I am from Italy.
2 you / Spain? / Are / from
   _____
3 are / Argentinian. / You / not
   _____
4 from? / you / Where / are
   _____
5 Canada. / am / from / I / not
   _____

2 Complete the conversations.

1 **A** Where _are_ you from?
   B I_'m_ from Madrid.

2 **A** Are you Polish?
   B Yes, I _____ .

3 **A** Are you from Mexico?
   B No, I _____ .

4 **A** _____ I in London?
   B No, you _____ . You _____ in Manchester!

5 **A** _____ you at university?
   B Sorry? Oh! _____ I a student? Yes, I _____ .

6 **A** _____ I in London, England?
   B No, you _____ . You _____ in London, Canada!

VOCABULARY

Numbers

1 Match the words to the correct numbers. There are four extra numbers.

30   15   11
62   97   100
9   31
20   ninety-seven
     thirty   fifteen
     eighty-five   twelve
64   sixty-two   thirty-one   13
     a hundred   seventy-four
     fifty-eight   forty-six
     eleven   nine   12
58   twenty-three
     74   26
46   85
     23

2 **CD T3** Listen and write the words.

1 _three_   5 _____
2 _____   6 _____
3 _____   7 _____
4 _____   8 _____

3 **Puzzle** Write the words in the puzzle.

1	8	fifteen	22
29		43	50
	64	71	
	92		106

How old are you?

4 **CD T4** Listen and complete the sentences.

1 I'm _fifty_ and I'm a teacher.
2 I'm _____ and I'm a student.
3 I'm not _____ . I'm _____ .
4 _____ are you?
   I'm _____ .
5 Sorry? Are you _____ ?
   No, I'm _____ !

PRONUNCIATION

/e/ /eɪ/

1 CD T5 Say the words. Then listen and repeat.

1 /e/
/ten/ ten
/frentʃ/ French

2 /eɪ/
/neɪm/ name
/speɪn/ Spain

2 CD T6 Say the words and complete the crossword. Then listen and check.

ACROSS ▶
3 /'neɪplz/
5 /'meksɪkəʊ/
6 /'twenti/

DOWN ▼
1 /twelv/
2 /kə'neɪdiən/
4 /eɪt/

```
         ¹W
    ²    W
³N A P L E S
              ⁴
         ⁵E    O
    I        G
⁶    E N      T
```

SURVIVAL ENGLISH

Greetings

1 CD T7 Put the conversations in the correct order. Then match the conversations with photos A and B. Listen and check.

One
a Hi, Ben. How are you? ☐
b Yes, I'm fine, thanks. ☐
c Afternoon, Helen! ☐ 1
d Fine, thanks. And you? ☐
Photo ___

Two
a I'm very well, thank you. And you? ☐
b Good morning, Mrs Smith. ☐
c Yes, I'm very well, thank you. ☐
d Good morning, John. How are you? ☐
Photo ___

2 Circle the correct response, a, b or c.

1 Morning, Sue.
  a Afternoon.
  b I'm fine, thanks.
  c Hi, Richard!
2 How are you?
  a I'm Jane.
  b I'm very well, thank you.
  c I'm from Berlin.
3 I'm fine, thanks. And you?
  a Yes, I'm fine.
  b Nice to meet you.
  c Good evening!

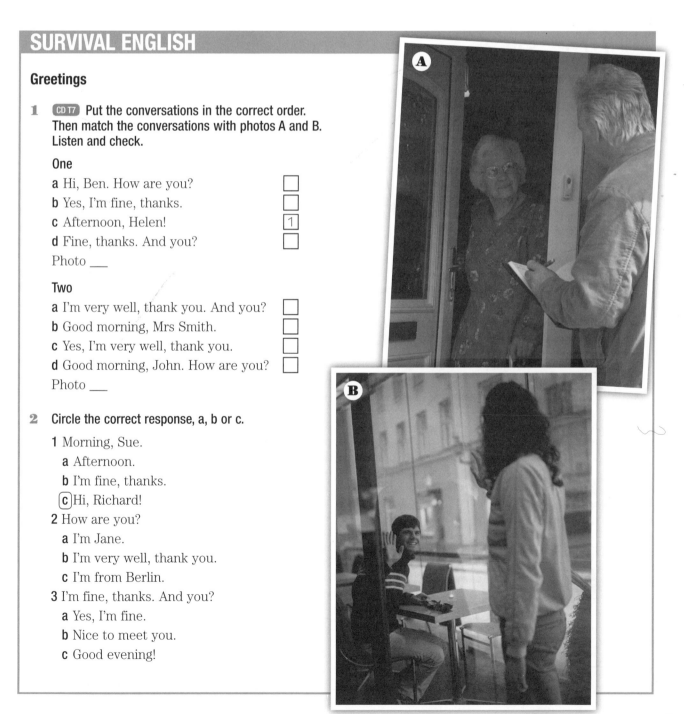

02 Jobs

GRAMMAR AND VOCABULARY

he/she, his/her

1 Complete the conversations.

1 A What's <u>his</u> name?
B His name's <u>Neil</u>.
A Where's <u>he</u> from?
B He's from <u>Ireland</u>.

2 A What's _____ name?
B Her name's _____.
A Where's _____ from?
B She's from _____.

3 A _____ name?
B His name's _____.
A _____ from?
B He's from _____.

4 A What's _____ name?
B Her _____.
A _____ from?
B She's _____.

5 A _____ name?
B _____ name's _____.
A _____ from?
B _____ from _____.

6 A _____?
B _____.
A _____?
B _____.

Vocabulary: jobs

2 Write the jobs.

1 c t a y r s e e r   _secretary_
2 c o r a t   _____
3 t r s i t e o e p i n c   _____
4 g s r e i n   _____
5 n e i e g n r e   _____

3 Write the jobs in the boxes.

①

② ☐☐☐☐☐☐☐

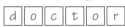

| d | o | c | t | o | r |

③ ☐☐☐☐☐☐
☐☐☐☐☐☐

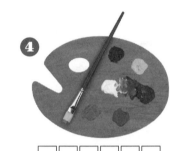

④ ☐☐☐☐☐

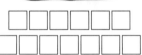

⑤ ☐☐☐☐☐☐☐

⑥ ☐☐☐☐☐

a/an

4 Write *a* or *an* in the correct place.

1 His name's Andy. He's ⌄ mechanic.   (a)

2 I'm from Poland. I'm engineer.

3 Marie's receptionist. She's from France.

4 Are you secretary?

5 Tom's actor from London.

6 Her name's Jill and she's artist.

***to be*: is/'s**

5 Write the sentences with *'s*.

1 Her name Katie.
  Her name's Katie.

2 Katie from London.
  _____

3 She a receptionist.
  _____

4 His name Bülent.
  _____

5 He an engineer.
  _____

6 Bülent Turkish.
  _____

he/she is, you are, your/his/her

6 Tick (✓) the correct sentence.

1 a She's a secretary.   ✓
  b She are a secretary.   ☐

2 a What's he's job?   ☐
  b What's his job?   ☐

3 a What's your name?   ☐
  b What's you're name.   ☐

4 a Where are you from?   ☐
  b Where she is from?   ☐

5 a How old is you?   ☐
  b How old is she?   ☐

6 a His job is an artist.   ☐
  b He's an artist.   ☐

7 Answer the questions about Mike Brown.

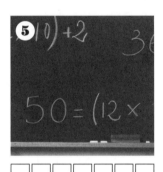

NAME:	Mike Brown
JOB:	Engineer
COUNTRY:	Canada
AGE:	22

1 What's his name?
  His name's Mike Brown.

2 What's his job?
  _____

3 Where is he from?
  _____

4 How old is he?
  _____

GRAMMAR AND LISTENING

to be: **is/isn't**

1 Look at the photos and complete the sentences with *'s/isn't*.

1 Jack <u>isn't</u> an engineer.
He _____ an actor.

2 Brigitte _____ Canadian.
She _____ French.

3 Miss Thomas _____ a doctor.
She _____ a teacher.

to be: **is** – questions and short answers

2 Write questions and short answers.

1 she / engineer?
<u>Is she an engineer</u> ?
<u>Yes, she is</u> . (+)

2 he / from Italy?
_____ ?
_____ . (−)

3 Miss Thomas / your teacher?
_____ ?
_____ . (−)

4 Jack / married?
_____ ?
_____ . (+)

5 your name / Alice?
_____ ?
_____ . (−)

3 Complete the questions.

1 <u>What's her name</u> ? Her name's Tania.
2 _____ Turkey? No, he isn't. He's from Argentina.
3 How _____ she? She's nineteen.
4 Where _____ ? He's from Poland.
5 _____ Bart? No, it isn't. His name's Brian.
6 _____ his _____ ? He's an artist.

VOCABULARY

Spelling: the alphabet

1 **CD T8** Listen and write the answers.

1 What's your name?
It's <u>Sheila. S-h-e-i-l-a</u> .
2 Are you German?
Yes, I'm from _____ .
3 Where's Rio de Janeiro?
It's in _____ .
4 Where's Peter from?
He's from _____ .
5 How old are you?
I'm _____ .
6 Is Maria Italian?
No, she's _____ .

2 **Puzzle** Complete the missing letters of the alphabet.

| a | | g | j | | p | | v | |

PRONUNCIATION

/ɑː/ /æ/

1 **CD T9** Say the words. Then listen and repeat.

   1 /ɑː/   **2** /æ/
   /frɑːns/ Fr<u>a</u>nce   /bæg/ b<u>a</u>g
   /ˈɑːtɪ̬st/ <u>a</u>rtist   /ˈkænədə/ C<u>a</u>nada

2 **CD T10** Put the words from the box in the correct column. Then listen and check.

<u>aren't</u> It<u>a</u>lian p<u>a</u>rdon D<u>a</u>n m<u>a</u>rried
M<u>a</u>rtin Sp<u>a</u>nish mech<u>a</u>nic <u>a</u>fternoon
th<u>a</u>nks

/ɑː/	/æ/
aren't	

3 Write sentences 1–4. Then tick (✓) the correct sentence, a or b.

   1 /jʊ/ /ɑːnt/ /ən/ /ˈɑːtɪ̬st/
   <u>You aren't an artist</u> .

   2 /dæn/ /ɪz/ /ˈmærɪd/
   _____ .

   3 /dæn/ /ɪz/ /ə/ /mɪˈkænɪk/
   _____ .

   4 /ˈmɑːtɪn/ /ɪz/ /ən/ /ˈɑːtɪ̬st/ /frəm/ /frɑːns/
   _____ .

   a Dan's an artist. ☐
   b Martin's from France. ☐

SURVIVAL ENGLISH

Excuse me …

1 **CD T11** Put the conversation in the correct order. Then listen and check.

   a It's a bank. ☐
   b Pardon? ☐
   c Oh, a bank! Sorry, I don't know. ☐
   d Excuse me. Where's HSBC? [1]
   e HSBC? I'm sorry, I'm from Germany. I don't understand. ☐
   f HSBC. ☐

2 Complete the conversations. Circle a, b or c.

   1 ___ Where's the bank, please?
      (a) Excuse me.
      b Pardon.
      c Good afternoon.

   2 Thank you very much.
      a I'm sorry.
      b I don't understand.
      c You're welcome.

   3 Are you Daniel Craig?
      a I don't know.
      b Pardon?
      c Excuse me.

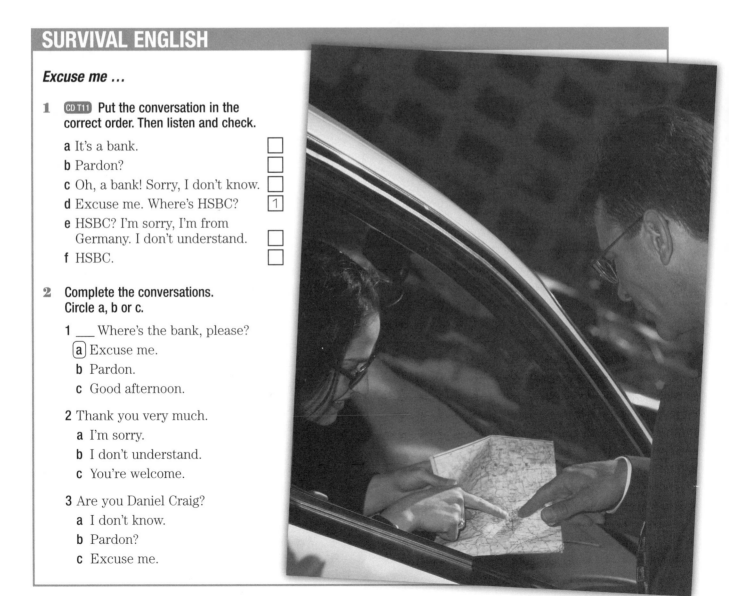

READING AND WRITING

His first name's Enrique and his surname's Morales. He isn't from the USA, he's from Puerto Rico. He's a singer, too.

She's American. She's from New York in the USA. She's a singer. Her first name's Alicia and her surname's Augello-Cook.

His first name's thomas and his surname is Mapother IV. he isn't a Singer, he's an Actor. he's from the usa.

florian Cloud de Bouinevialle Armstrong isn't american. she isn't French. she's from london, england. she's a Singer.

1 Look at the photos and read texts A–D. Match names 1–4 to the texts.

1 Tom Cruise — C
2 Ricky Martin — ☐
3 Dido — ☐
4 Alicia Keys — ☐

2 Read the box and look at texts A and B. Tick (✓) the correct answers.

We use capital letters for:	
• countries (England)	✓
• nationalities (English)	☐
• jobs	☐
• names (Mary, London)	☐
• I (I am)	☐
• to start a sentence	☐

3 Correct texts C and D.

4 Write four or five sentences about a person (a friend/singer/actor). Use texts A–D to help you.

Penelope Cruz is from Spain. She …

10

SELF-ASSESSMENT TEST 1 | UNITS 1–2

1 Put the words from the box in the correct column. (5 points)

~~Turkey~~ French American Canada Germany Italian

Countries	Nationalities
Turkey	

2 Match the numbers to the words. (5 points)

25 56 8 40 15 12
33 67 ~~71~~ 94 100

1 seventy-one _71_
2 fifty-six ____
3 fifteen ____
4 thirty-three ____
5 twenty-five ____
6 a hundred ____
7 twelve ____
8 forty ____
9 ninety-four ____
10 eight ____
11 sixty-seven ____

3 Complete the jobs. Write *a* or *an*. (5 points)

1 <u>a s i n g e r</u>
2 _ w _ _ _ e r
3 _ _ e _ _ _ t _ _ y
4 _ _ _ g _ _ _ e r
5 _ m _ _ _ a _ _ c
6 _ _ e _ _ _ t _ _ n _ _ t

4 Circle the correct answer, a, b or c. (5 points)

1 ___ a secretary.
  a Her b Your **c** She's

2 What's ___ job?
  a his b he's c she

3 What's ___ name?
  a he's b your c she

4 Where's ___ from?
  a he b I c her

5 How old is ___ ?
  a you b she c he's?

6 ___ an artist.
  a I'm b His c Your

5 Write the sentences. (5 points)

1 He / singer.
  He's a singer .

2 Anna / police officer.
  _____

3 She / Polish.
  _____

4 Adam / electrician.
  _____

5 Her name / Helen.
  _____

6 She / from Russia.
  _____

6 Put the words in the correct order to make sentences. (5 points)

1 a / is / waiter. / He
  He is a waiter .

2 Kelly / actor. / isn't / Mr / an
  _____

3 not / engineer. / I / an / am
  _____

4 teacher / Mrs / your / Is / Thomas?
  _____

5 is / a / Tim / from / mechanic / Ireland.
  _____

6 from / You / not / France. / are
  _____

Total ___ /30

I know	Yes	No	?
• to be: am/'m not/am I?	☐	☐	☐
• to be: are/aren't/are you?	☐	☐	☐
• to be: is/isn't/is he?	☐	☐	☐
• my/your/his/her	☐	☐	☐
• I/you/he/she/it	☐	☐	☐
• a/an	☐	☐	☐

03 Family life

GRAMMAR AND READING

Vocabulary: family

1 Find eight more family words. Look → and ↓.

g	b	s	i	s	t	e	r
r	e	b	i	e	g	f	k
a	i	l	w	s	m	a	m
n	f	h	h	c	o	j	b
d	a	u	g	h	t	e	r
p	t	s	b	i	h	u	o
a	h	b	s	l	e	n	t
r	e	a	o	d	r	a	h
e	r	n	w	r	y	g	e
n	d	d	g	e	v	x	r
t	z	q	p	n	e	o	k
s	o	n	y	f	w	a	s

Plural nouns

2 Complete the sentences with the correct words.

1 His <u>brothers</u> aren't doctors, they're <u>musicians</u>. (musicians/brothers)
2 Helen and I aren't _____. She's my _____. (friend/sisters)
3 Her _____ is a teacher but her sons are _____. (actors/daughter)
4 My mum's a _____ and my uncles are _____. (engineers/secretary)
5 Are your _____ _____ or singers? (artists/children)

to be: are/aren't

3 Write the sentences.

1 artists / Manchester/ from /we (+)
  <u>We are artists from Manchester</u>.
2 Emma / her / and / David / children (−)
  <u>Emma and David aren't her children</u>.
3 son / daughter / and / students / my (+)
  _____.
4 and / musicians / brothers / Paul / his (−)
  _____.
5 big / from / a / family / you (−)
  _____.
6 sister / his / teachers / and / husband / her (+)
  _____.

to be: questions

4 Write the questions.

1 <u>Are you happy in Oxford</u>?
  Yes, we're very happy in Oxford.
2 _____?
  We're from New York.
3 _____?
  No, they aren't Mexican. My grandparents are Polish.
4 _____?
  I'm eighteen and my brother's twenty.
5 _____?
  No, we aren't students. We're singers.
6 _____?
  My mother's from Germany but my father's Spanish.

to be: is/isn't, are/aren't

5 Complete the text with the correct form of *to be*.

Shiloh ¹<u>is</u> from a famous family. She ²_____ from New York, she's from New Orleans! Her surname ³_____ Jolie-Pitt. Her mother ⁴_____ Angelina Jolie and her father ⁵_____ Brad Pitt. They ⁶_____ American actors. Her sister and brother ⁷_____ famous, too. They ⁸_____ from America, they're from Africa and Asia! Her brothers Maddox and Pax ⁹_____ from Cambodia and Vietnam. Her sister Zahara ¹⁰_____ from Ethiopia. Maddox, Zahara and Pax ¹¹_____ American but Shiloh is. Together they are one big happy family!

GRAMMAR AND LISTENING

Vocabulary: family

1 Write the words for Tim's family.

                    Tim
1 Becky   sister
2 Carol and Bernard   _____
3 Helen   _____
4 Peter   _____
5 Nora   _____
6 Bernard   _____

Possessive 's

2 Replace *his/her* with the name in the brackets and possessive *'s*.

1 His family isn't very big. (Tim)
   <u>Tim's family isn't very big</u>.
2 Peter is her uncle. (Becky)
   _____
3 Her grandmother is short. (Gemma)
   _____
4 His parents aren't American. (Tim)
   _____
5 His wife is from New York. (Peter)
   _____
6 Her daughter is Gemma's aunt. (Helen)
   _____

3 Circle the possessive *'s*.

1 My sister(s) sons are short.
2 Bill is her husband's brother.
3 His father's an engineer.
4 Her family's Spanish.
5 Jack's a great actor.
6 Where are Jim's parents from?
7 Are they Susan's photos?
8 It's a very big wedding.

4 Puzzle Who's who? Complete the sentences.

> Jane's Freddy's mother.
> Kate's Jane's sister.
> Harry's Kate's husband.
> Barbara's Kate's mother.

1 Harry is Freddy's <u>uncle</u>.
2 Kate's Freddy's _____.
3 Freddy's Jane's _____.
4 Jane's Barbara's _____.
5 Barbara is Freddy's _____.

Possessive adjectives

5 Complete the table.

Subject pronouns	Possessive adjectives
I	my
	your
he	
	her
we	
they	

6 Complete the conversation with words from Exercise 5.

A What are ¹ _your_ names?
B I'm Jacques and this is ² _____ sister.
³ _____ name's Michelle.
A Are you from France?
B Yes, ⁴ _____ are. ⁵ _____ parents are from Paris.
A What are ⁶ _____ jobs?
B My dad's a musician and ⁷ _____ mum's a housewife.
A Is your dad in a band?
B Yes, ⁸ _____ band's name is Cubana.
A You're tall. Are ⁹ _____ parents tall, too?
B No, ¹⁰ _____ aren't!

LISTENING

1 CD T12 Listen. Tick (✓) true and cross (✗) false.

Emily
1 Emily's mum has got a brother. ✓
2 Emily's grandmother has got three children. ☐

Lily
3 Lily's husband is German. ☐
4 Lily's husband has got a sister. ☐

Freddy
5 Freddy's mother isn't from Manchester. ☐
6 Freddy's uncle comes from Berlin. ☐

Elizabeth
7 Frank's wife is a teacher. ☐
8 Elizabeth has got two children and two grandchildren. ☐

VOCABULARY AND GRAMMAR

Irregular nouns

1 Complete the sentences with plural nouns.

1 John and Fred's _wives_ are sisters. (wife)
2 Two of my teachers are _____ . (man)
3 The _____ in the photo are doctors. (woman)
4 Three _____ in my class are musicians. (person)
5 David and Janet are their _____ . (child)

Adjectives

2 Complete the sentences with adjectives from the box.

<del>small</del> poor sad new
big bad old good

1 It's _small_ .
2 She's _____ .
3 She's _____ .

4 He's _____ .
5 It's _____ .

6 They're _____ .
7 He's _____ .
8 It's _____ .

Adjectives and plural nouns

3 Complete the sentences with adjectives and plural nouns.

1 His mother is tall but he's s h o r t .
2 Their father's car is old and very u _ _ _ .
3 My friend's sisters are pretty w _ _ _ _ .
4 English p _ _ _ _ _ are very polite.
5 We aren't a t _ _ _ family.
6 They aren't bad c _ _ _ _ _ _ _ .

PRONUNCIATION

/æ/ /ʌ/

1 **CD T13** Say the words. Then listen and repeat.

1 /æ/
/dæd/ d<u>a</u>d
/ˈfæməli/ f<u>a</u>mily

2 /ʌ/
/mʌm/ m<u>u</u>m
/ˈʌŋkəl/ <u>u</u>ncle

2 **CD T14** Listen and number the words 1–12. Listen again and repeat.

/ˈʌgli/ [1]   /ˈhæpi/ [ ]   /mʌðə/ [ ]
/bæd/ [ ]   /sʌn/ [ ]   /ˈlʌndən/ [ ]
/ˈbrʌðə/ [ ] /ˈæktə/ [ ]   /ˈhʌzbənd/ [ ]
/ˈspænɪʃ/ [ ] /ˈrʌʃə/ [ ] /bæg/ [ ]

3 **CD T15** Say the sentences. Then listen and repeat.

1 Her mum's from Russia.
2 My uncle's in London.
3 His son's car is ugly.
4 He's a bad actor.
5 My husband's Spanish.
6 Their brother's my dad.

SURVIVAL ENGLISH

Saying goodbye

1 Complete gaps 1–6 for situations in pictures A–C. Use words and phrases from the box.

<s>Bye</s> Goodbye Take
Goodnight See you

A Bye Jack!
B ¹ <u>Bye</u> , Harry. ² _____ _____ later.

A Goodnight, mum.
B ³ _____ , Sam. Sleep well.

2 Circle the correct response, a or b.

1 Goodnight, Tom. Sleep well.
   ⓐ Goodnight. See you tomorrow.
   b Bye. See you later.

2 Bye, Joe. See you later.
   a And you.
   b Bye, Liz. Take care.

3 Bye, dad.
   a Goodbye, Ann. Take care.
   b Goodnight. See you.

A Bye, dad.
B ⁴ _____ , Jane. ⁵ _____ care.

04 Places

GRAMMAR AND READING

Vocabulary: places

1 Match places 1–13 in Bigsby to the words in the box.

bank [3] café [ ] church [ ]
cinema [ ] club [ ] hospital [ ]
hotel [ ] library [ ] museum [ ]
park [ ] post office [ ] supermarket [ ]
theatre [ ]

there is/isn't/are/aren't

2 Complete the sentences about Bigsby.

1 <u>There's</u> only one <u>cinema</u> in Bigsby.
2 _____ _____ two _____ _____ .
3 _____ _____ some supermarkets and three _____ .
4 _____ _____ a theatre or a park.
5 _____ _____ a lot of clubs and cafés.
6 _____ _____ _____ hospitals.

a, some, a lot of, any

3 Circle the correct answers.

1 There's *some* / *a* bank in this town.
2 There aren't *any* / *some* museums.
3 There are *a* / *some* libraries.
4 There isn't *a lot of* / *a* good hotel here.
5 There are *a* / *a lot of* great theatres.
6 There aren't *any* / *some* churches.

there is/ isn't/ are/ aren't

4 Write sentences. Use the prompts with *a*, *some* or *any*.

1 hotel (+) restaurants (−)
   There's a hotel. There aren't any restaurants.
2 supermarket (+) café (−)
   _____
3 cinema (+) theatres (−)
   _____
4 libraries (+) university (−)
   _____
5 post office (+) banks (−)
   _____
6 museums (+) clubs (−)
   _____
7 parks (+) buses (−)
   _____

Adjectives

5 Complete the sentences with the correct adjective.

1 Your town is g r e a t ! There are lots of theatres and clubs.
2 My town is very b _ _ _ _ _ . There isn't a cinema or a good restaurant.
3 There's a good museum with i _ _ _ _ _ _ _ _ _ _ photos of the old town.
4 The park in the centre is very n _ _ _ , it has a fountain and lots of lovely trees.
5 The traffic in my city is t _ _ _ _ _ _ _ ! There are lots of cars everywhere!
6 The cafés and restaurants in my town are simply f _ _ _ _ _ _ _ _ ! You can always eat delicious food there!

6 Complete the sentences about pictures 1–4.

There's only one _____ in the town.

_____ _____ some great _____ .   _____ _____ nice theatres.

_____ _____ a lot of _____ .

LISTENING

1 **CD T16** Listen and tick (✓) the true sentences. Then correct the false sentences.

1 Jerry's parents are Italian. ✓
   _____
2 Jerry's a teacher at Columbia University. ☐
   _____
3 The university is near Times Square. ☐
   _____
4 There aren't any good theatres or clubs there. ☐
   _____
5 The museums are very boring. ☐
   _____
6 The restaurants are terrible. ☐
   _____

GRAMMAR AND VOCABULARY

Vocabulary: shops and facilities

1 Write the names of places 1–9 on the plan.

is/are there?

2 Complete the questions about Marston town centre.

1 <u>Are there</u> any burger bars?
2 _____ a museum?
3 _____ any bookshops?
4 _____ a supermarket?
5 _____ any telephones?
6 _____ any record shops?

is there/are there: short answers

3 Write questions and short answers about Marston.

1 she / engineer?
  <u>Is there a church in the town centre</u>?
  <u>No, there isn't</u>.
2 toilets / on Black Street?
  _____?
  _____.
3 post office / on Henry Street?
  _____?
  _____.
4 telephones / in the town centre?
  _____?
  _____.

PLAN OF MARSTON TOWN CENTRE

RITZ HOTEL

9 _____ SHOP

8 _____

CINEMA

1 <u>shoe</u> SHOP

ALBERT SQUARE

HENRY STREET

2 _____ _____

3 _____ SHOP

7 _____ _____

4 _____

LIBRARY

6 _____ SHOP

BLACK STREET

POST OFFICE

5 _____

4 **Correct the mistake in each sentence.**

1 Is there some bank on this street?
  Is there a bank on this street?
2 There is an internet café in the town?
  _____
3 Is there any bookshops on London Road?
  _____
4 Are there some good burger bars in New York?
  _____
5 Is there any bookshops here?
  _____
6 There are any nice parks in London?
  _____

VOCABULARY

Prepositions of place

1 **Complete the conversations about Marston with the words from the box.**

on (x 4)   opposite (x 2)   next to (x 2)
the left   the right   in

1 **A** Excuse me. Where's the library?
  B It's ¹ *on* Albert Square. It's ² _____
  _____ the sports shop.
2 **A** Sorry. Is there a bookshop ³ _____
  Black Street?
  B Yes, it's ⁴ _____ the post office, on
  ⁵ _____ _____ .
3 **A** Excuse me. Is there an internet café
  ⁶ _____ the town?
  B Yes, it's ⁷ _____ Henry Street, ⁸ _____
  the cinema.
4 **A** Where's Brown's, the clothes shop, please?
  B It's ⁹ _____ Albert Square, on ¹⁰ _____
  _____ . It's ¹¹ _____ _____ the
  burger bar.

2 **Puzzle Read and answer the question.**

**The bookshop is next to the sports shop.
The sports shop is opposite the post office.
The cinema is next to the post office.
What's opposite the cinema?**

PRONUNCIATION

/ɒ/ /əʊ/

1 **CD T17 Say the words. Then listen and check.**

  1 /ɒ/   2 /əʊ/
  /ʃɒp/ shop   /həʊˈtel/ hotel
  /ɒn/   on   /nəʊ/   no

2 **CD T18 Put the words from the box in the correct column. Then listen and check.**

job office clothes sorry post only
don't opposite know hospital

/ɒ/	/əʊ/
job	

SURVIVAL ENGLISH

Asking for and giving directions

1 **Complete the conversations with the words from the box.**

where far near (x 2) on know
over (x 2) next there opposite

1 **A** Excuse me. ¹ *where*'s the museum?
  B It's ² _____ there ³ _____ the right
  It's ⁴ _____ to the café.
  A Thank you!
2 **A** Excuse me. Is ⁵ _____ a hospital
  ⁶ _____ here?
  B I'm sorry, I don't ⁷ _____ !
  A That's OK.
3 **A** Excuse me. Are there any telephones
  ⁸ _____ here?
  B Yes, they're not ⁹ _____ . They're
  ¹⁰ _____ there, ¹¹ _____ the
  King's Hotel.

2 **Write a short dialogue. Give directions to a place near your school/home.**

  A Excuse me. Where's the library?
  B _____
  _____
  _____

READING AND WRITING

1 Read the emails and circle the correct answers a or b.

1 Who's happy in Bath?
   a Amelia   b Pietro

2 Who's far from the city centre?
   a Amelia   b Pietro

2 Read the emails again. Tick (✓) the true sentences.

1 Amelia's school is very good. ✓
2 Her English family's house is not far from the city centre. ☐
3 There are a lot of interesting clubs in Bath. ☐
4 Pietro's school's very small. ☐
5 There are a lot of interesting museums. ☐
6 There are some good restaurants in Bath. ☐

3 Read the box and match 1–5 with a–e. Underline examples in Amelia's email.

Punctation
1 , [c]   2 ! ☐   3 ' ☐   4 ? ☐   5 's ☐
a question mark
b possessive 's
c comma
d apostrophe
e exclamation mark

4 Correct Pietro's email.

Hi Antonio,
Bath's boring. The school's terrible …

5 Imagine you're in an English school in Bath. Write an email to a friend. Use the emails and pictures here to help you.

Hi Peter,
I'm in Bath! It's …

SELF-ASSESSMENT TEST 2 | UNITS 3–4

1 Add five words in each column. (5 points)

Family	Places
daughter	church

2 Replace the underlined adjective with the opposite adjective from the box. (5 points)

~~ugly~~   rich   terrible   short   interesting   new

1 Their town is very pretty <u>ugly</u>.
2 Her uncle is <u>boring</u> _____.
3 Is your mother very <u>tall</u> _____?
4 There's a nice, <u>old</u> _____ hotel here.
5 There are some <u>fantastic</u> _____ bookshops here.
6 His grandparents are very <u>poor</u> _____.

3 Circle the correct answer, a or b. (5 points)

1 Our parents are very nice ___.
   a persons   **b** people
2 The ___ in my family are very pretty.
   a woman   b women
3 It's over there, on the ___.
   a left   b opposite
4 My grandson is a very happy ___.
   a child   b children
5 The restaurant is ___ the cinema.
   a on the right   b next to
6 The hotel's ___ the church.
   a near to   b opposite

4 Complete the sentences with possessive 's, or *is* in the correct place. (5 points)

1 My mum ∧'s family ∧is very big.
2 Her uncle wife from New York.
3 Her husband father a teacher.
4 Carol daughter very pretty.
5 Jack girlfriend Spanish.
6 Their sister son a student.

5 Write negative sentences using the word in brackets. (5 points)

1 There's a restaurant on Park Street. (café)
   <u>There isn't a café on Park Street</u>.
2 There are a lot of bookshops in the town. (supermarkets)
   _____.
3 They're mechanics. (engineers)
   _____.
4 There's a theatre here. (cinema)
   _____.
5 We're from Scotland. (Ireland)
   _____.
6 There are some nice clothes shops near here. (shoe shops)
   _____.

6 Write questions 1–6. Match the questions to answers a–f. (5 points)

1 your aunt / an artist?
   <u>Is your aunt an artist</u>? [c]
2 their grandparents / from here?
   _____? [ ]
3 How many / churches / in Bath?
   _____? [ ]
4 any good clothes shops / near here?
   _____? [ ]
5 an Internet café / in the town centre?
   _____? [ ]
6 Where / the toilets, / please?
   _____? [ ]

a No, there isn't.
b They're over there.
~~c No, she isn't.~~
d No, they aren't.
e Yes, there are some great shops in Oxford Street.
f I don't know. There are a lot!

Total ____ /30

I know	Yes	No	?
• *to be*: you/we/they; are/aren't?	☐	☐	☐
• there is/isn't/are/aren't?	☐	☐	☐
• a/some/a lot of/any	☐	☐	☐
• you/we/they; your/our/their	☐	☐	☐

21

05 Likes and dislikes

GRAMMAR AND READING

Vocabulary: verbs

1 Complete the gaps with the verbs from the box.

~~work~~ play have live eat speak

1 _work_ — in a shop / in Manchester / in a library
2 _____ — pizza / Italian food / a lot
3 _____ — Russian / three languages / very fast
4 _____ — football / tennis / for England
5 _____ — a computer / a job / two brothers
6 _____ — in London / with my family / in the centre

Present Simple: I/you/we/they

2 Complete the sentences with verbs from Exercise 1.

1 I _don't speak_ three languages. (−)
2 They _____ a nice car. (+)
3 We _____ a lot of pizzas. (+)
4 You _____ in a library. (−)
5 They _____ for Manchester United. (−)
6 We _____ with our parents. (+)

3 Complete the sentences about the pictures 1–6.

We _don't like_ bananas.

You _____ a lot of burgers.

They _____ a car.

I _____ in Rome.

They _____ in a shop.

We _____ tennis.

4 Write true sentences about you.

| I | (don't) | work / live / eat / have / play / like / speak | with my friends. / in a record shop. / tennis. / coffee. / Italian. / a sister. / Mexican food. |

1 _I don't work in a record shop_ .
2 _____ .
3 _____ .
4 _____ .
5 _____ .
6 _____ .

Present Simple: questions and short answers

5 Write the questions and answers.

1 you / live / Manchester?
  <u>Do you live in Manchester</u> ?
  Yes, <u>I do</u> .
2 they / eat / Chinese food?
  _____ ?
  No, _____ .
3 your parents / work / in the centre?
  _____ ?
  No, _____ .
4 they / have / any brothers and sisters?
  _____ ?
  Yes, _____ .
5 you / speak / three languages?
  _____ ?
  Yes, I _____ .
6 we / have / any coffee?
  _____ ?
  No, we _____ .

Present Simple: all forms

6 Complete the conversation.

Michelle Hi! I'm Michelle.
Ergun Hi. My name's Ergun. I'm from Turkey.
Michelle ¹<u>Do</u> you live in Istanbul?
Ergun No, I ²_____ . I live in Ankara. And you?
Michelle I'm Canadian.
Ergun Really? Where ³_____ you live? Toronto?
Michelle No, I ⁴_____ in Montreal. We speak French there.
Ergun You ⁵_____ fantastic English, too. What's your job?
Michelle I ⁶_____ have a job. I'm a student. ⁷_____ you work?
Ergun Yes, I ⁸_____ . I'm a mechanic.
Michelle ⁹_____ you like your job?
Ergun Yes, I do!

GRAMMAR AND SPEAKING

Vocabulary: sports, free time, food

1 Label the pictures and add one more word in each category.

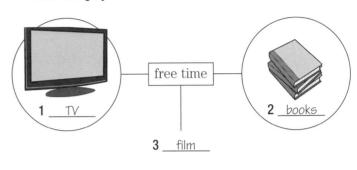
1 <u>TV</u> free time 2 <u>books</u>
3 <u>film</u>

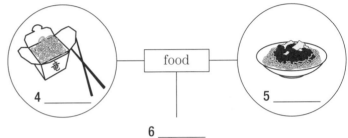
4 _____ food 5 _____
6 _____

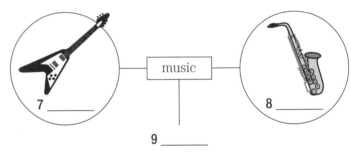
7 _____ music 8 _____
9 _____

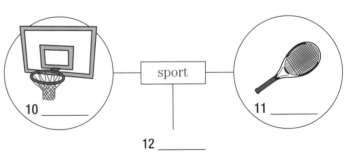
10 _____ sport 11 _____
12 _____

Likes and dislikes

2 Complete the sentences with the correct words. Use the symbols to help *you*.

1 I <u>really like</u> hospital programmes on TV. 👍☺
2 We _____ basketball. 😐
3 My mum and dad _____ Italian food. ♥
4 I _____ boring films. ☹
5 My friends _____ hip hop. ☹👎
6 They _____ classical music. 👍☺

23

Object pronouns

3 Complete the table with the words from the box.

~~me~~ him you them it us

Subject pronouns	Object pronouns
I	me
	you
he	
she	her
	it
we	
they	

4 Write the sentences with the correct object pronoun.

1 We don't play football. We hate ~~football~~.
    We don't play football. We hate it.

2 I quite like Brad Pitt. Do you like Brad Pitt?
    _____

3 I love hip hop but my friends hate hip hop.
    _____

4 We don't eat vegetables. We don't like vegetables.
    _____

5 They play tennis with my brother and me.
    _____

6 Dido is a great singer. I love Dido.
    _____

5 Complete the sentences with object pronouns.

1 Do you eat a lot of bananas?
    Yes, we really like *them* .

2 Do your sisters like your boyfriend?
    No, they hate _____ .

3 Is that a photo of _____ ?
    Yes. I'm with my friends.

4 Do you like Susan?
    Well, I quite like _____ .

5 Do you play basketball?
    No, I don't like _____ .

6 Do you like _____ ?
    Yes, I love you!

VOCABULARY

Food and drink

1 Find thirteen more food and drink words. Look → and ↓.

h	a	m	b	u	r	g	e	r	v	x	t
c	h	o	c	o	l	a	t	e	e	d	a
a	w	r	h	i	o	p	u	g	l	m
s	q	a	e	o	x	c	v	b	e	k	f
m	i	n	e	r	a	l	w	a	t	e	r
i	t	g	s	p	f	d	s	a	a	c	u
l	y	e	e	l	t	e	a	g	b	z	i
k	a	j	p	c	o	l	a	y	l	p	t
d	y	u	r	c	h	i	c	k	e	n	w
h	f	i	s	h	o	e	g	g	s	h	o
v	b	c	r	t	y	p	o	i	u	j	f
r	t	e	a	g	a	r	c	h	i	p	s

PRONUNCIATION

/ʃ/ /tʃ/ /dʒ/

1 **CD T19** Say the words. Then listen and repeat.

1 /ʃ/
    /fɪʃ/   fi<u>sh</u>
    /ʃiː/   <u>sh</u>e

2 /tʃ/
    /tʃɪps/ <u>ch</u>ips
    /tʃiːz/ <u>ch</u>eese

3 /dʒ/
    /ˈɒrɪndʒ/ oran<u>g</u>e
    /dʒuːs/   <u>j</u>uice

2 **CD T20** Listen and number the words, 1–12.

/ʃuː/	1	/tʃɜːtʃ/	☐
/endʒɪˈnɪə/	☐	/ˈtʃɪkɪn/	☐
/ʃɒp/	☐	/ˈlæŋɡwɪdʒ/	☐
/ˈdʒɜːmən/	☐	/ˈtʃɒklɪt/	☐
/rɪˈsepʃənɪst/	☐	/ˈtɜːkɪʃ/	☐
/ˈsænwɪdʒ/	☐	/ˈvedʒtəbəlz/	☐

3 **Puzzle** Read the sentences. What do they eat?

1 Charlie and Sharon
    /ˈtʃɑːli/ /ənd/ /ˈʃærən/ /heɪt/ /fɪʃ/
    /bət/ /ðeɪ/ /lʌv/ /ˈvedʒtəbəlz/

2 Jane and John
    /dʒeɪn/ /ənd/ /dʒɒn/ /laɪk/ /ˈtʃɒklɪt/
    /bət/ /ðeɪ/ /dəʊnt/ /laɪk/ /tʃɪps/

SURVIVAL ENGLISH

Prices

1. **CD T21** Listen and write the prices.

   1. £1.60   5. _____
   2. _____   6. _____
   3. _____   7. _____
   4. _____   8. _____

2. Write the prices from Exercise 1 in words.

   1. one pound sixty
   2. _____
   3. _____
   4. _____
   5. _____
   6. _____
   7. _____
   8. _____

3. **CD T22** Listen to the conversation and complete the prices on the menu.

   ### Ricky's Café
   MENU

   Food
   Sandwiches
     egg, cheese, chicken   ¹£2.20
   Hamburger and chips   £4.00
   Chicken and vegetables   £4.50
   Egg and chips   £2.40
   Chocolate cake   ² _____

   Drinks
   Tea   90p
   Coffee   ³ _____
   Mineral water   ⁴ _____
   Cola   80p
   Fruit juices   ⁵ _____

Ordering and buying food

4. Put the words in the correct order to make the conversations.

   Anna please. / and / chips, / Egg
   ¹ Egg and chips, please .

   Man else? / Anything
   ² _____.

   Anna Yes. / cake / and / A / please. / a / cola, / chocolate
   ³ _____.

   Man are. /you / Here
   ⁴ _____.

   Anna is / How / that? / much
   ⁵ _____.

   Man pounds / please. / four / That's / seventy,
   ⁶ _____.

5. Write a conversation for *you*. Use the menu from Exercise 3.

   You Hello. ¹_____, please.
   Man Sure. Anything else?
   You Yes. ²_____, please.
   Man Here you are.
   You ³_____?
   Man That's ⁴_____, please.

06 Routines

GRAMMAR AND VOCABULARY

LARA'S DAY

1 Lara <u>wakes up</u> late.

2 She _____ fruit and coffee for breakfast.

3 She _____ home at 1 p.m.

4 She _____ work at 4 in the afternoon.

5 She _____ work at 11.

6 She _____ home at 12 at night.

7 She _____ to bed at 2 in the morning.

Present Simple: *he/she/it*

1 Look at pictures 1–7. What's Lara's job? Complete the sentences with the verbs from the box.

<u>wake up</u> finish get go
have leave start

2 Complete more sentences about Lara. Use the correct verb in the right form.

1 Lara <u>wakes up</u> at 10 a.m. (wake up/start)
2 She _____ her Spanish class at 2 in the afternoon. (go/start)
3 She _____ to work at 4 in the afternoon. (get/leave)
4 She _____ dinner at the hotel. (go/eat)
5 She _____ the hotel at 11 p.m. (get to/ leave)
6 She _____ to bed late. (go/finish)

3 Complete the sentences with the correct verb from the box.

~~go~~   finish   play   relax   eat   study

1 She _goes_ to school at 8.
2 My brother _____ basketball at school.
3 She _____ French in the afternoon.
4 My dad _____ work at 6 p.m.
5 He _____ a hamburger and chips for lunch.
6 My mother _____ with a book after dinner.

usually/sometimes/never

4 Put the words in the correct order to make sentences.

1 mum / up / at / My / wakes / 7. / usually
   My mum usually wakes up at 7 .
2 leave / sometimes / 5 p.m. / They / school / at
   _____ .
3 never / 2 p.m. / has / at / He / lunch
   _____ .
4 sandwich / for / a / lunch. / usually / He / eats
   _____ .
5 friend / at / sometimes / My / night. / studies / late
   _____ .
6 never / sons / school. / play / at / Her / football
   _____ .

5 Write the sentences from Exercise 4 about *you*.

1 _I never wake up at 7_ .
2 _____ .
3 _____ .
4 _____ .
5 _____ .
6 _____ .

6 Correct the sentences.

1 She usually eat fish and chips on Friday.
   She usually eats fish and chips on Friday .
2 Lara doesn't usually has coffee for breakfast.
   _____
3 My friends they never play tennis.
   _____
4 We usually starts work early.
   _____
5 Robert wears sometimes a uniform.
   _____
6 I doesn't never get to work late.
   _____

GRAMMAR AND LISTENING

Present Simple: *he/she/it*

1 Complete the sentences about the pictures with the verbs in brackets.

Sheila _works_ in a bank. (work)
She doesn't work in a bookshop.

Mr Smith _____ near the hospital. (live)
_____ near the church.

Michelle _____ chicken. (like)
_____ vegetables.

David _____ basketball. (play)
_____ football.

Annie _____ English. (study)
_____ Chinese.

Mario _____ a sandwich for lunch. (have)
_____ a pizza for lunch.

2 Tick (✓) the correct sentence.

1 a She not goes to work on Saturdays. ☐
  b She doesn't go to work on Saturdays. ✓
2 a Tom doesn't work in a bank. ☐
  b Tom work in a bank. ☐
3 a They don't eat Chinese food. ☐
  b They don't never eat Chinese food. ☐
4 a My teacher doesn't like chocolate. ☐
  b My teacher really like chocolate. ☐
5 a My brothers aren't play basketball. ☐
  b My brothers don't play basketball. ☐
6 a We lives in Canada. ☐
  b We don't live in Canada. ☐

Present Simple: questions

3 Complete the conversations.

1 What ¹_does_ Lorna do?
   She ²_works_ in a record shop.
   ³_____ she wear a uniform?
   Yes, she ⁴_____ .
   ⁵_____ she like her job?
   Yes, she ⁶_____ . She loves it!

2 What ¹_____ Kevin do ?
   He ²_____ in a bank.
   ³_____ he _____ a uniform?
   No, ⁴_____ _____ .
   ⁵_____ he _____ his job?
   No, he ⁶_____ . He hates it!

LISTENING

1 CDT23 Listen to Isabel. Circle the correct answer, a or b.

1 Isabel comes from ___ .
   a England   b Mendoza
2 In Mendoza, shops are open ___ .
   a in the evening   b in the afternoon
3 Isabel ___ sleeps in the afternoon.
   a sometimes   b usually
4 Isabel's brother ___ school at 2.
   a starts   b finishes
5 Her sister ___ gets up early.
   a usually   b never
6 Isabel's family usually has dinner ___ .
   a at 7   b at 11

VOCABULARY AND SPEAKING

Days of the week

1 Put the letters in the correct order to make days of the week. Number them 1–7 in the correct order.

1 a o d y m n   _Monday_ [1]
2 a e y s d u t _____ ☐
3 y h d u t s a r _____ ☐
4 d a y r t a s u _____ ☐
5 d r f a y i   _____ ☐
6 n d d y w e s e a _____ ☐
7 a u n y s d   _____ ☐

Telling the time

2 Match the times to the words.

1 5.15   a twenty-five to eight   [c]
2 6.50   b twenty past eight   ☐
3 7.35   c quarter past five   ☐
4 11.30   d quarter to ten   ☐
5 8.20   e ten to seven   ☐
6 9.45   f half past eleven   ☐

3 CD T24 Listen and draw the times.

1   2   3

4   5   6

4 Puzzle Complete the bus times and the two sentences below.

BUS 205				
6.30	6.55			8.10
	9.00	9.25		

1 Bus 205 leaves every _____ minutes.
2 The last bus leaves at _____ .

Prepositions – at/on/in

5 Complete the sentences with at, on, in.

1 I usually go to the cinema _on_ Friday night.
2 We never get up early ___ the weekend.
3 Do you work ___ the evening?
4 Lara sometimes finishes work ___ 11.30.
5 They usually study ___ night.
6 Does he play football ___ Saturday afternoon?

PRONUNCIATION

/ɜː/ /ɔː/

1 **CD T25** Say the words. Then listen and check.

1 /ɜː/
/wɜːk/ w<u>or</u>k
/'ɜːli/ <u>ear</u>ly

2 /ɔː/
/fɔː/ f<u>our</u>
/spɔːt/ sp<u>or</u>t

2 **CD T26** Complete the crossword. Then listen and check.

ACROSS ▶
2 /'bɜːgə/
4 /ʃɜːt/
5 /'fɔːti/
7 /'mɔːnɪŋ/
8 /'sætədeɪ/

DOWN ▼
1 /'kwɔːtə/
2 /'bɔːrɪŋ/
3 /'θɜːzdeɪ/
6 /'θɜːti/

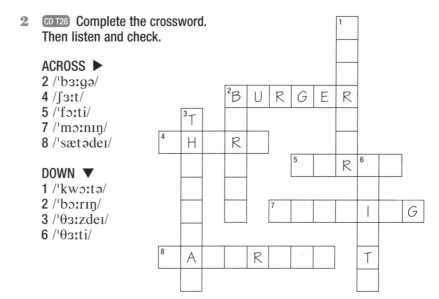

SURVIVAL ENGLISH

Talking about time

1 **CD T27** Listen to four conversations. Match them to texts A–D.

1 [C] 2 [ ] 3 [ ] 4 [ ]

2 **CD T27** Complete the conversations with sentences a–f. Then listen and check.

1 A ¹ _e_
B At ten past two.
A Thank you.

2 A What time does John's train arrive?
B ² ___

3 A Excuse me. Is there a post office near here?
B Yes, it's over there, next to the library.
A ³ ___
B I think it closes at 1 on Saturday.

4 A ⁴ ___
B There's *Friends* at 8. Then there's a film.
A ⁵ ___
B ⁶ ___

a What time does it start?
b At 9 o'clock.
c When does it close?
d What's on TV tonight?
e ~~What time does the bus leave Oxford, please?~~
f It arrives at quarter past six.

3 Write two more conversations. Use texts C and D.

1 A What time does the bus from Oxford arrive in London?
B _____

2 A _____
B _____

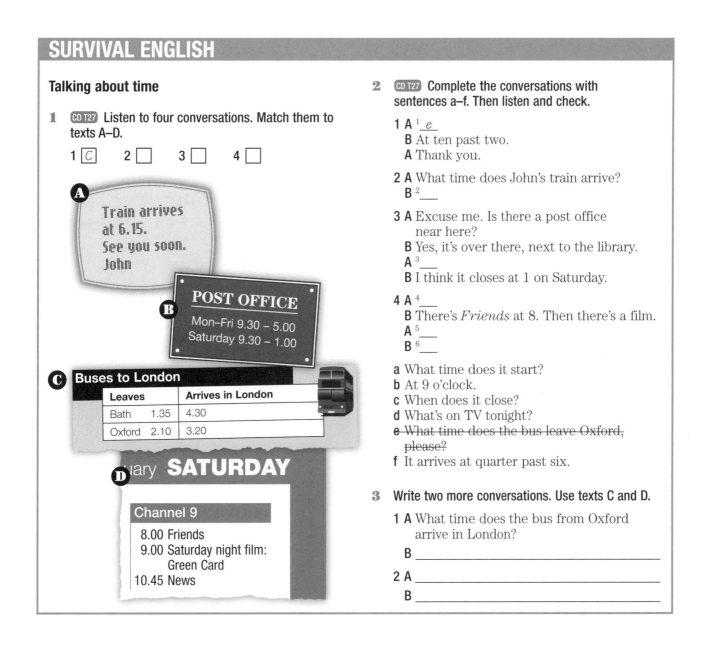

READING AND WRITING

FUTURE CHAMPION?

A Who is she?
Sasha is seventeen. She's from Russia but now she lives in Florida. She goes to a tennis school near Miami.

B What does she do?
She's a tennis player. She gets up very early and plays tennis from 8 to 12. In the afternoon, she has normal school lessons and studies English.

C What does she eat?
She eats fruit, vegetables and fish. She eats a lot of bananas but she never has chocolate cake.

D What does she like?
She likes jazz and pop music but she doesn't like hip hop and rock. She quite likes TV but her favourite thing is … shopping!

E What about the future?
She wants to be famous and play at Wimbledon. Good luck, Sasha!

1 Read the text and write short answers to the questions about Sasha.

1 Where does she live now?   _Florida._
2 What does she do in the morning? _____
3 Does she eat fast food? _____
4 What music does she like? _____
5 What's her favourite thing? _____
6 What does she want to do in the future?
_____

2 Read the text again and complete the box.

and or *but*?	
1 She gets up early ___and___	c
2 She likes jazz _____	☐
3 She eats fruit, vegetables _____	☐
4 She's from Russia _____	☐

a now she lives in Florida.
b fish.
c plays tennis from 8 to 12.
d she doesn't like hip hop.

3 Join the sentences. Use *and* or *but*.

1 She likes vegetables. She hates turkey.
   She likes vegetables but she hates turkey.

2 He works on Saturday. He doesn't work on Sunday.
   _____

3 We love rock music. We love jazz.
   _____

4 I speak English. I speak Chinese. I speak Swedish.
   _____

5 They play football. They don't play basketball.
   _____

4 Write about Thomas. Use the notes to help *you*.

Who is he?
Poland / Cracow / 18.
What does he do?
Mon-Fri, 9-5: university student
Sat-Sun: football.
What does he eat?
hamburgers, chips ♥
chicken, vegetables ☹
What does he like?
films, books, classical music 👍☺
jazz, pop and rock, TV ☹👎
What about the future?
play football / Chelsea!

Thomas is from Poland and he lives in …

30

SELF-ASSESSMENT TEST 3 | UNITS 5–6

1 Put the words from the box in the correct column. (3 points)

~~cola~~ Monday hip hop chicken
Thursday jazz milk films cheese
eggs evening Tuesday books
afternoon tea basketball

Food and drink	Music and free time	Days and times of the day
cola		

2 Write the times. (2 points)

1 4.15 quarter past four
2 2.20 _____
3 3.25 _____
4 7.45 _____
5 11.55 _____

3 Complete the sentences with the correct prepositions. (5 points)

1 I play tennis _at_ the weekend.
2 He gets up ___ 12 ___ Sunday.
3 My sister leaves home ___ 8 ___ the morning.
4 We don't go ___ school ___ Saturday afternoon.
5 They go ___ bed late ___ Friday.
6 Do you have dinner ___ 10 o'clock ___ night?

4 Complete the sentences with *usually*, *sometimes* or *never*. (5 points)

1 We _sometimes_ eat fast food. We quite like it.
2 We _____ start work at 8.30 but on Saturday we start at 10.
3 She _____ eats vegetables. She hates them.
4 I _____ have orange juice for breakfast. I love it.
5 He's a mechanic. He _____ wears a suit at work.
6 I usually study in the evening but I _____ go out with my friends.

5 Complete the answers with a verb and an object pronoun. (5 points)

1 Do you like David?
   Yes, I really _like him_ .
2 Does Pete eat chicken?
   No, he never _____ .
3 Do they like the Spice Girls?
   Yes, they really _____ .
4 Do you eat fish?
   Yes, we usually _____ on Friday.
5 Does he speak French.
   Yes, he _____ a lot in his job.
6 Does her brother like you?
   No, he doesn't _____ at all!

6 Write the questions and complete the answers. (10 points)

1 you / work / in Oxford?
   Do you work in Oxford ?
   Yes, _we do_ .
2 Where / Suzy and George / live?
   _____?
   _____ in New York.
3 your grandparents / speak Polish?
   _____?
   No, _____ .
4 your brother / like jazz?
   _____?
   No, _____ . _____ hip hop.
5 What languages / you and your sister / speak?
   _____?
   _____ Spanish and English.
6 Annie / play basketball?
   _____?
   Yes, she _____ and tennis, too!

Total ☐ /30

I know	Yes	No	?
• Present Simple:			
I/you/we/they go/don't go.	☐	☐	☐
He/she/it goes/doesn't go.	☐	☐	☐
Do I/Does he go …?	☐	☐	☐
• usually/sometimes/never	☐	☐	☐
• me/you/him/her/it/us/them	☐	☐	☐

07 Talent

GRAMMAR AND LISTENING

Vocabulary: jobs

1 What are their jobs? Put the letters in the correct order.

Jake is a great _guitarist_ . (arutsitig)

Emma is a bad _____ . (rgsnie)

Jack and Jill are good _____ . (tiivslosin)

Nick and Anne are great _____ . (enadrsc)

Tom is a bad _____ . (nitiasp)

Steve is a boring _____ . (ocrta)

can/can't

2 Complete the sentences about the pictures with *can* or *can't*.

1 Jake _can_ play the guitar.
2 Emma _can't_ sing.
3 Jack and Jill _____ play the violin.
4 Nick and Anne _____ dance.
5 Tom _____ play the piano.
6 Steve _____ act.

3 Complete the conversations with the correct form of *can*. Match the correct picture (from 1–6) to each conversation.

A ☐

A ¹ _Can_ you play a musical instrument?
B Yes, of course, I ² _____ . I ³ _____ play the saxophone very well but I ⁴ _____ play the piano – I'm a terrible pianist.

B ☐

A So what do you want to be?
B I want to be a singer. I ⁵ _____ sing really well.
A ⁶ _____ you sing for us now?
B Yes, I ⁷ _____ but I ⁸ _____ sing without my guitar …
A So you ⁹ _____ sing without an instrument?
B No, I ¹⁰ _____ .

C ☐

A ¹¹ _____ your friends dance?
B Oh, yes they ¹² _____ . They ¹³ _____ dance every night and never get tired at all!

32

can: questions and short answers

4 Write questions and answers about David, Anna and Kate.

	David	Anna	Kate
sing	✓	✗	✗
dance	✗	✓	✓
play the piano	✗	✓	✓
speak Spanish	✓	✗	✓
play basketball	✗	✓	✓
act	✓	✗	✗

1 David / sing?
   Can David sing ?
   Yes, he can .

2 he / play basketball?
   _____ ?
   _____ .

3 he / speak Spanish?
   _____ ?
   _____ .

4 Anna and Kate / dance?
   _____ ?
   _____ .

5 they / sing and act?
   _____ ?
   _____ .

6 Anna / play the piano?
   _____ ?
   _____ .

5 Write true sentences about *you*, your family and friends.

1 My best friend can't dance.
2 My _____ speak English.
3 I _____ play the violin
4 My _____ play basketball.
5 I _____ sing.

GRAMMAR AND READING

Vocabulary

1 Circle the correct word.

1 Can he *perform* / drive a go-kart?
2 She's a very *fit* / *funny* comedian.
3 Can you *teach* / *learn* me to cook?
4 My mum sometimes cooks a new *dish* / *dinner* at the weekend.
5 Our teacher usually *asks* / *asks for* our opinions in class.
6 They never laugh at his sense of *humour* / *jokes*.

have to/has to

2 Complete the sentences with *have to/has to*.

1 My dad has to drive to work.
2 I _____ cook lunch.
3 My sister _____ study a lot at college.
4 We _____ learn English at school.
5 A sports teacher _____ be very fit.
6 Actors _____ perform in front of people.
7 You _____ study a lot to get to university.
8 It's very late for the children. They _____ go to bed now.

don't/doesn't have to

3 Write the sentences with *don't/doesn't have to* and the verbs from the box.

do laugh at be cook
go wake up have go

1 I don't have to do sports at college.
2 Racing drivers _____ a sense of humour.
3 You _____ my brother's jokes.
4 She _____ to college in the morning.
5 A violinist _____ fit.
6 An actor _____ early in the morning.
7 I _____ to school, it's Sunday!
8 We _____ today. We're going out to a restaurant.

have to/has to, don't/doesn't have to

4 Complete the text. Use the verbs in the box and the correct form of *have to*.

~~go~~ (not) take know start walk
(not) work (not) walk

Daniel is a student and he ¹ *has to go* to college from 9.30 to 4. But in his free time he's a dog walker. He ² _____ early – he takes four dogs to the park in the morning and six dogs in the evening. He ³ _____ them for an hour. He ⁴ _____ very hard but he gets a lot of money – £100 a week! And he ⁵ _____ the dogs at the weekend! Daniel says, 'I ⁶ _____ exams for this job – but I ⁷ _____ a lot about dogs!'

have to/has to: questions and short answers

5 Write questions and short answers about Daniel and his job.

1 Daniel / go / to college at 9.30?
   Does Daniel have to go to college at 9.30 ?
   Yes, he does .

2 he / walk dogs / in the afternoon?
   _____ ?
   _____ .

3 he / work at the weekend?
   _____ ?
   _____ .

4 dog walkers / take exams?
   _____ ?
   _____ .

5 they / know a lot / dogs?
   _____ ?
   _____ .

VOCABULARY AND SPEAKING

Adjectives and adverbs

1 Write the adverbs for these adjectives.

adjective	adverb
loud	loudly
slow	
quiet	
fast	
bad	
good	

2 CD T28 Listen and write the correct adverb in sentences 1–6.

1 My dad always laughs very *loudly* .
2 Tom's usually late and he drives very _____ .
3 Susie practises the piano _____ when her son's asleep.
4 He's famous and he plays football very _____ .
5 She always speaks _____ on the phone so I can understand her.
6 He isn't a good musician. He plays the violin very _____ .

3 Circle the correct word.

1 I'm not a very good cook. I cook very (*badly*) / *bad*.
2 The children have to play *loud / quietly* after lunch.
3 She can't sing but she dances very *good / well*.
4 He's a very boring comedian. He speaks very *quiet / slowly*.
5 Her boyfriend loves go-karting. He drives very *slow / fast*.
6 My brothers play *loud / loudly* music every night.

LISTENING

1 **CD T29** Listen and write the correct adverb in the box.

Mark …	How?
plays basketball	very badly
plays tennis	
speaks English	
plays the guitar	
sings	
drives	

PRONUNCIATION

/b/ /v/

1 **CD T30** Say the words. Then listen and check.

1 /b/
/bæd/ bad
/bʊk/ book

2 /v/
/ˌvaɪəˈlɪn/ violin
/ˈnevə/ never

2 **Puzzle** Write the sentences.

A Are _____?
B Yes, terrible! _____!

SURVIVAL ENGLISH

Requests

1 Complete the dialogues with phrases from the box.

<del>Can you repeat</del>   Can you speak
Can I help   Can I have
Can you help   Where can I

1 **A** That's fifteen fifty.
  B Sorry. ¹ *Can you repeat* that, please?
  A It's fifteen pounds fifty pence.

2 **A** ² _____ you?
  B Yes. ³ _____ a coffee, please?

3 **A** ⁴ _____ me, please?
  B Sure. What's the problem?
  A ⁵ _____ buy some stamps?
  B They sell them in the post office. It's over there.

4 **A** Sorry, I don't understand.
  ⁶ _____ slowly, please?
  B OK. The post office is over there.

2 Complete the phone call with sentences a–d.

A ¹ _c_
B No, sorry, he's out.
A ² ___
B Sure.
A ³ ___
B Laura's in the Café Roma. OK.
A ⁴ ___
B Bye.

a Can you give him a message, please?
b Thank you. Goodbye.
c <del>Hello. Can I speak to Mark, please?</del>
d It's Laura. I'm in the Café Roma.

08 Free time

GRAMMAR AND READING

Vocabulary: collocations

1. Match two words or phrases from the box to each verb 1–6.

   a hat   an email   a dog   loudly   a T-shirt
   on the phone   a postcard   orange juice
   hard   children   coffee   in a clothes shop

   1 wear   a hat   a T-shirt
   2 talk   _____   _____
   3 work   _____   _____
   4 drink _____   _____
   5 write _____   _____
   6 play with _____ _____

Present Continuous

2. Complete the sentences with verbs from Exercise 1.

   1 I 'm wearing my new jeans.
   2 My friend _____ (play) with his dog.
   3 You _____ (talk) on the phone again!
   4 They are busy. They _____ (write) emails.
   5 My mum _____ (work) hard.
   6 We are in a café and we _____ (drink) very good coffee.

3. Look at the picture and write sentences. Use the Present Continuous.

   1 John / wear …
      John's wearing a T-shirt .
   2 Bill and Martha / write …
      _____.
   3 Emily / drink …
      _____.
   4 Tania / eat …
      _____.
   5 Steve and Jimmy / play …
      _____.
   6 Joe / work …
      _____.

Present Continuous: negative

4 Look at the picture and make these sentences negative.

1 John is reading a book.
   <u>No, John isn't reading a book</u>.
   <u>He's reading a newspaper</u>.
2 Billy and Martha are writing emails.
   _____.
   _____.
3 Joe is drinking coffee and relaxing.
   _____.
   _____.
4 Tania is eating a cake.
   _____.
   _____.
5 Steve and Jimmy are playing the piano.
   _____.
   _____.
6 Emily's son is sleeping now.
   _____.
   _____.

Present Continuous

5 Correct the sentences.

1 He playing the piano at the moment.
   <u>He is playing the piano at the moment</u>.
2 Look! They are drive my car!
   _____.
3 We writing postcards now.
   _____.
4 She not cooking lunch at the weekend.
   _____.
5 I am not talk to a friend on the phone now.
   _____.
6 He isn't drive his car at the moment.
   _____.

GRAMMAR AND LISTENING

Vocabulary: rooms and furniture

1 Look at the pictures and complete the phrases with furniture names.

1 a <u>table</u> and four _____

2 a _____ and a small _____

3 a _____ and a big _____

4 two _____ and an _____

5 a _____ and a _____

2 Complete words 1–9 in the table.

Room	Furniture
¹ <u>living room</u>	sofa, ²a_____ , ³c_____ , ⁴<u>t</u>_____
kitchen	⁵<u>f</u>_____ , ⁶<u>c</u>_____
⁷<u>b</u>_____	bed
⁸<u>b</u>_____	shower, ⁹<u>t</u>_____

Present Continuous: questions and short answers

3 Complete the questions about photos 1–4. Write short answers.

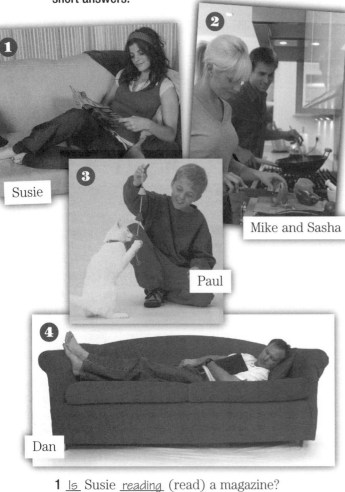

1 Is Susie _reading_ (read) a magazine?
   Yes, she is.
2 ____ Mike and Sasha _____ (eat) lunch?
   _____
3 ____ Paul _____ (play) with the cat?
   _____
4 ____ Dan _____ (using) the computer?
   _____

4 Write the questions and the answers about photos 1–4.

1 Susie / study?
   Is Susie studying ?
   No, she's reading a magazine .
2 Mike and Sasha / eat / sandwiches?
   _____?
   No, _____.
3 Paul / watching / a video?
   _____?
   No, _____.
4 Dan / read / a book?
   _____?
   No, _____.

5 Complete the phone call. Use the Present Continuous.

James   Hi, Louise. It's me!
Louise Hi, James. How are you?
James   Fine. ¹_Are_ you _eating_ (eat)?
Louise Yes, I ²_____ ! I'm at home. I ³_____ dinner with my sister.
James   ⁴_____ you _____ (have) curry?
Louise No, we ⁵_____ . Sorry, James! We ⁶_____ (eat) a big pizza! What ⁷_____ you _____ (do)?
James   I ⁸_____ (study) but it's boring. Can I come and have some pizza, too?
Louise Yes, sure!
James   Great! See you soon.

VOCABULARY

1 Write the verbs from the box in the correct place. There are two extra verbs.

~~watch~~   play   surf   listen   do   read   have   visit

1 _watch_ DVDs / a film
2 _____ a book / a magazine
3 _____ a shower / fun
4 _____ basketball / the violin
5 _____ to music / to CDs
6 _____ friends / relatives

2 Complete the sentences with the words from the box.

~~relatives~~   the newspaper   a bath   the radio   the Internet   a football match

1 He's phoning his _relatives_ .
2 We're watching _____ .
3 My sister's having _____ .
4 I surf _____ every day.
5 He usually listens to _____ .
6 Are you reading _____ ?

3 **Puzzle** What rooms are they in?

> Ben's mum is cooking dinner. She's talking to his dad. His brother's having a shower and his sister's reading a book on her bed. Their dog's sleeping on the sofa. Ben isn't in his bedroom or the kitchen. He's watching TV.

1 Ben's parents   _kitchen_
2 His brother   _____
3 His sister   _____
4 The dog   _____
5 Ben   _____

PRONUNCIATION

/w/ /v/ /f/

1 [CD T31] Say the words. Then listen and check.

1 /w/
/wɔːk/ walk
/ˈʃaʊə/ shower

2 /v/
/ˈvɪzɪt/ visit
/ˌtiː ˈviː/ TV

3 /f/
/ˈfʌni/ funny
/fəʊn/ phone

2 [CD T32] Complete the crossword. Then listen and check.

ACROSS ▶
4 /ˈwɔːtə/
5 /frɪdʒ/
7 /lɑːf/
8 /diː viː ˈdiː/
9 /ˈiːvnɪŋ/

DOWN ▼
1 /ˈsəʊfə/
2 /ˈvɪdiəʊ/
3 /ˌwiːkˈend/
4 /weə/
6 /wɒtʃ/

SURVIVAL ENGLISH

Making arrangements

1 [CD T33] Put the conversation in the correct order. Then listen and check.

a No, I don't. Why?
b Yes – great!
c Do you have any plans for tomorrow afternoon? **1**
d OK. Let's meet at 2.30.
e In the café near the stadium.
f OK. See you tomorrow.
g There's a concert on at the football stadium. Do you want to go?
h Where?

2 Circle the correct answer, a, b or c.

1 Are you free this afternoon?
 a Tonight.
 (b) Yes, I am.
 c Great!
2 Do you want to go shopping?
 a Good idea!
 b I'm not.
 c See you.
3 Let's meet at 8 o'clock at my house.
 a Why?
 b See you tomorrow!
 c OK. See you later!

3 Write a dialogue. Invite a friend to *one* of the events below. Use the conversation in Exercise 1 help you.

READING AND WRITING

1 Read postcard 1 from Jessica to her mum and dad. Answer the questions.

1 Where is she now?
   <u>She's in Rome now</u>.
2 What's she doing?
   _____.
3 What are her friends doing?
   _____.
4 Can she speak good Italian?
   _____.
5 What does she have to do now?
   _____.

2 Replace the words in *italics* with the correct pronoun. Then check in postcard 1.

> We use **pronouns** (*it, they, them*) to join our ideas.
>
> **1a** Hello from Rome! *Rome*'s a beautiful city. I love *Rome*.
> **1b** Hello from Rome! _____ a beautiful city. I love _____!
> **2a** And the Italians are great – I *love the Italians*, too!
> **2b** And the Italians are great – I love _____, too!

3 Match the <u>underlined</u> words in postcard 1 to *a* and *b* below.

a Italian language
b some Italian friends

1

Dear Mum and Dad,
Hello from Rome! It's a beautiful city. I love it! And the Italians are great – I love them, too! I'm writing this postcard in a café in the Piazza di Spagna. I'm with some Italian friends from my class. <u>They</u>'re practising their English and I'm learning Italian! I can't speak it very well but I love <u>it</u>. The university is very good and I'm studying a lot! I have to go to classes now. Write soon
lots of love,
Jessica

Mr and Mrs P. Smith,
17 New Street,
Smalltown,
B11 57D
England / Ingilterra

2

Hi Harry!
Ciao from Roma! I'm not studying at the moment – I'm sitting in a café. <u>The café</u> is in the Piazza di Spagna. <u>The Piazza di Spagna</u> is very romantic! I'm with an Italian friend. <u>My Italian friend</u> is practising his English. <u>My Italian friend</u> doesn't speak <u>English</u> very well. The university is great. I love <u>the university</u>. I go to parties and clubs every night. <u>The parties and clubs</u> are great! I'm having lots of fun but I'm not working very hard – don't tell my mum and dad!
Write soon!
Jess xxx

Harry Jones,
21 Old Street,
Smalltown,
B11 34H
England / Ingilterra

4 Read postcard 2. Tick (✓) correct and cross (✗) false.

1 Jessica is writing to her parents. ✗
2 She's with an Italian friend. ☐
3 She's practising her Italian. ☐
4 Her friend speaks English very well. ☐
5 She doesn't like parties or clubs. ☐
6 She doesn't study very hard. ☐

5 Write postcard 2 again. Replace the <u>underlined</u> words with pronouns.

SELF-ASSESSMENT TEST 4 | UNITS 7–8

1 Complete the crossword with furniture words. (5 points)

Across: 3 CH_R, 4 T B, 5 B
Down: 1 TOILET, 2 FR_R, 3 CHO_R

2 Complete the words. (5 points)

1 Richard's a musician. He plays the **v i o l i n**.
2 I usually have a **s _ _ _ _ _** before breakfast.
3 I speak Russian very **b _ _ _ _**.
4 You have to learn to **d _ _ _ _** a car.
5 We can't **c _ _ _** but we can eat a lot!
6 She's a **g _ _ _ _ _ _ _ _** in a rock band.

3 Write one more word for each verb. (5 points)

1 **learn** French, _languages_
2 **write** a postcard, _____
3 **talk** quietly, _____
4 **have** a shower, _____
5 **listen** to music, _____
6 **watch** TV, _____
7 **read** a book, _____
8 **wear** a T-shirt, _____
9 **visit** friends, _____
10 **phone** a friend, _____
11 **work** fast, _____

4 Complete the sentences with a verb from the box and *can/have to*. (5 points)

~~play~~   dance   cook   do   speak   be

1 My friends _can play_ the guitar. (can)
2 _____ you _____ your homework now? (have to)
3 Their uncle _____ any languages. (can't)
4 You _____ fit to be a racing driver. (have to)
5 _____ you _____ very well? (can)
6 You _____ dinner tonight. (not have to)

5 Correct the mistake in each sentence. (5 points)

1 He's listening music.
   He's listening to music.
2 They can't to play football.
   _____
3 Do you want to go to cinema?
   _____
4 They surfing the Internet again?
   _____
5 I have study for a test now.
   _____
6 Do you playing the violin at school?
   _____

6 Write the questions. Then match them to answers a–f. (5 points)

1 you / are / doing / now? / What
   What are you doing now? [c]
2 Is / English / she / school? / learning / at
   _____ [ ]
3 walking / the / Are / dog? / they
   _____ [ ]
4 you / have / When / to / do / go?
   _____ [ ]
5 playing / Where / they / are / tonight?
   _____ [ ]
6 you / have / this / to / do / evening? / What / do
   _____ [ ]

a No, they aren't.
b At 8.30.
c ~~I'm playing with my sister's children.~~
d I have to study for a test.
e At the Boreton football stadium.
f Yes, she is.

Total ☐ /30

I know	Yes	No	?
• can/can't/can I/?	☐	☐	☐
• have to/has to; don't/doesn't have to; do they/does he have to?	☐	☐	☐
• Present Continuous: am/is/are + verb-ing	☐	☐	☐

41

09 Changes

GRAMMAR AND VOCABULARY

was/wasn't/were/weren't

1 Circle the correct answer about the people in the photos.

1 Elvis Presley *was* / *wasn't* American.
2 Benny Hill *was* / *wasn't* a singer.
3 Ayrton Senna and Juan Fangio *wasn't* / *weren't* comedians.
4 Edith Piaf *was* / *wasn't* from France.
5 Anna Pavlova and Rudolph Nureyev *were* / *weren't* dancers.
6 Groucho Marx *wasn't* / *weren't* from Brazil.

2 Complete the sentences.

1 Edith Piaf <u>wasn't</u> a Russian dancer.
2 Benny Hill and Anna Pavlova _____ from the USA.
3 Ayrton Senna _____ from Brazil.
4 Groucho Marx and Elvis Presley _____ Russian.
5 Juan Fangio _____ an Argentinian dancer.
6 Rudolph Nureyev and Anna Pavlova _____ from Russia.

was/were: questions and short answers

3 Write the questions and answers.

1 Benny Hill / the USA?
<u>Was Benny Hill from the USA</u> ?
<u>No, he wasn't</u> .

2 Edith Piaf / a French singer?
_____?
_____ .

3 Fangio and Senna / racing drivers?
_____?
_____ .

4 Elvis Presley / a singer / England?
_____?
_____ .

5 Pavlova and Nureyev / American dancers?
_____?
_____ .

6 Groucho Marx / a comedian / Russia?
_____?
_____ .

Juan Manuel Fangio
Argentinian
racing driver

Ayrton Senna
Brazilian
racing driver

Groucho Marx
American
comedian

Benny Hill
English
comedian

Anna Pavlova
Russian
dancer

Rudolph Nureyev
Russian
dancer

Edith Piaf
French
singer

Elvis Presley
American
singer

Vocabulary

4 Complete the sentences with the words from the box.

~~player~~   videos   record   cassette
radio   songs

1 His new CD _player_ was a birthday present.
2 My mum always has her portable _____ next to her bed.
3 We don't usually buy _____ now. We buy DVDs.
4 Their grandfather was very proud of his old LPs and _____ player.
5 I have 2000 _____ and 500 photos on my MP4.
6 Some people still listen to music on their portable _____ players.

Time expressions

5 Complete the sentences with *on* if necessary.

1 I was in bed at 10 o'clock _–_ last night.
2 He was at school ___ this morning.
3 We were at the shopping centre ___ Sunday afternoon.
4 Were you at your English class ___ yesterday?
5 They weren't at home ___ Saturday night.
6 I wasn't here ___ last year. I was in the USA with my family.

6 Complete the sentences to make them true for *you*. Use the phrases from the table.

1 I _wasn't at home last night._
2 My friends _____
3 My brother _____
4 My sister _____
5 My parents _____

Where	When
at school / home at the cinema / the shopping centre at a party / a club in bed / a café	last night on Friday night yesterday on Saturday afternoon last weekend on Sunday evening

READING AND VOCABULARY

Years

1 [CD T34] Listen and write the years in numbers. Then write them in words.

1 _1981_   _Nineteen eighty-one_
2 _____   _____
3 _____   _____
4 _____   _____
5 _____   _____
6 _____   _____

Adjectives

2 Put the letters in the adjectives 1–9 in the correct order.

In 1965 I was sixteen, the Beatles were famous and it was a ¹_g r e a t_ (traeg) time to be young. Record players were the new fashion in technology. They weren't small, cheap and ²_____ (sglsoy) black like today's MP3s – they were very big, ³_____ (evpesinxe) and in ⁴_____ (tfdneiref) colours. My record player was red and grey. I was very proud of it – it was ⁵_____ (tcperfe)! The mini-skirt was the new fashion in clothes – it was very ⁶_____ (ralupop). All my clothes were black. It wasn't a ⁷_____ (usseoir) colour for me and my friends then – it was ⁸_____ (omedrn)! Yes, 1965 was a ⁹_____ (cinaattsf) year!

3 Write the names of things/places in your town or country.

1 a popular song   _____
2 a glossy magazine   _____
3 a serious newspaper   _____
4 a modern building   _____
5 an amazing place   _____
6 a cheap restaurant   _____

VOCABULARY

Colours and seasons

1 Find six colours across → and four seasons down ↓.

b	g	r	e	y	r	t	y	w	p
s	z	x	c	v	b	n	m	i	l
p	s	q	w	a	r	s	d	n	f
r	u	g	h	u	w	h	i	t	e
i	m	j	k	t	l	w	a	e	z
n	m	x	c	u	v	b	y	r	u
g	e	a	t	m	p	m	n	o	e
b	r	o	w	n	q	t	r	e	d
s	f	s	i	l	v	e	r	g	s
c	e	r	y	b	l	a	c	k	u

2 Circle the noun that *doesn't* match the adjective.

green car flower dog
pink tree sky guitar
orange car banana sofa
blue vegetable sky T-shirt
gold medal tree telephone
yellow fruit vegetable cloud

3 Complete the sentences about *you*. Use colours.

When I was 10, my favourite …

1 … fruit was yellow (banana) .
2 … T-shirt was _____ .
3 … vegetable was _____ .
4 … flowers were _____ .
5 … food was _____ .
6 … drink was _____ .

4 Write the season for each picture.

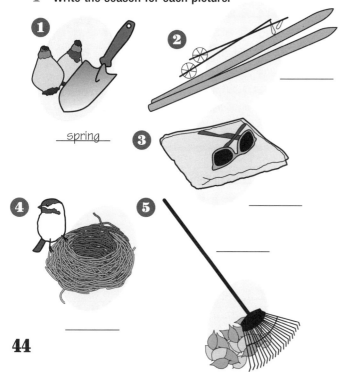

1 _____ 2 _____
  spring
3 _____
4 _____ 5 _____

VOCABULARY AND LISTENING

Months and ordinal numbers

1 Write the months. Then order them first to twelfth.

1 ruyanja   January   first
2 ljyu   _____ _____
3 ruyberfa   _____ _____
4 meerpsteb   _____ _____
5 rnbomvee   _____ _____
6 amy   _____ _____
7 meebdrce   _____ _____
8 guusta   _____ _____
9 rmahc   _____ _____
10 neju   _____ _____
11 tberooc   _____ _____
12 iarlp   _____ _____

Dates

2 **CD T35** Listen and complete the dates.

1 the twenty-fourth of March
2 the _____ of December
3 the eleventh of _____
4 the _____ of May
5 the _____ of February
6 the twelfth of _____

3 Write the dates.

1 15/06 the fifteenth of June
2 21/08 _____
3 03/09 _____
4 25/12 _____
5 01/01 _____
6 12/07 _____

4 Complete the sentences about *you*.

1 My birthday's on 26th September .
2 Our summer holidays are in _____ .
3 Our last English test was on _____ .
4 I was born in _____ . (year)
5 Our last holiday was in _____ . (place)

5 **Puzzle** Read about Sam and answer the question.

> Sam's 24th birthday was on the last day in February in 2008. His true birthday is every four years.

When was he born? Write the date.

_____

PRONUNCIATION

Sentence stress: was/were

1 **CD T36** Listen and repeat the sentences.

1 /wəz/
Was he at school?
No, he was at home.

/wə/
Were they at home?
No, they were at school.

2 /wɒz/
Where was he?
He wasn't at home.

/wɜː/
Where were they?
They weren't at school.

2 **CD T37** Listen and tick (✓) the pronunciation of was/were in each sentence.

	/wəz/	/wɒz/	/wə/	/wɜː/
1	✓			
2				
3				
4				
5				
6				
7				
8				

SURVIVAL ENGLISH

Talking about dates

1 Complete the conversation with sentences a–e.

A Where were you in this photo, Annie?
B ¹ *We were in France on a family holiday* .
A When was it?
B ² _____ .
A How old were you? Seven?
B ³ _____ .
A And how old were you when Liz was born?
B ⁴ _____ .
A So you were nine in this photo!
B ⁵ _____ .

a No, I wasn't. My sister Liz was seven.
b Yes, I was!
c ~~We were in France on a family holiday.~~
d I was two.
e In 1998.

2 Complete the conversation with the words from the box.

wasn't   birthday   ~~were~~   where
when (x 2)   was   born

A ¹ *Were* you born in Scotland, Alistair?
B No, I ² _____ . But my father ³ _____ .
A ⁴ _____ is he from? Edinburgh?
B No, Glasgow.
A Oh! My dad's from Glasgow, too.
B Is he? ⁵ _____ was he born?
A In 1971.
B My dad was ⁶ _____ in 1971, too!
A Really? ⁷ _____ is his birthday?
B On the 21st of July.
A That's amazing!
B Why? Is your dad's ⁸ _____ on the 21st of July?
A No, but it's *my* birthday!

3 Write questions and answers about Bill Gates and his family.

When was Bill Gates born? He was born on …

Name	Bill Gates
Born	Seattle, USA – 28 October 1955
Wife	Melinda French Gates
Born	Dallas, USA – 15 August 1964
Children	Jennifer (1996), Rory (1999), Phoebe (2002)

45

10 Travel

GRAMMAR AND READING

Past Simple regular verbs: spelling

1 Write the verbs in the past tense.

1 walk — walked
2 decide — _____
3 study — _____
4 like — _____
5 phone — _____
6 play — _____
7 marry — _____
8 stop — _____
9 travel — _____
10 look — _____

-ed endings: pronunciation

2 Put the verbs from Exercise 1 in the correct column.

/d/	/t/	/ɪd/
	walked	

3 Complete the sentences with the verbs from the box. Use the Past Simple.

~~sail~~   arrive   stop   stay   travel   study

1 They _sailed_ ten thousand kilometres in a small boat.
2 The strong winds _____ after three hours.
3 We _____ across the USA for two months.
4 It was very late when he _____ home.
5 I _____ English for three hours before dinner.
6 She _____ in a cheap hotel when she was in London.

GRAMMAR AND SPEAKING

Past Simple: irregular verbs

1 Find the past forms of verbs 1–8. Look → and ↓ in the box.

1 ~~do~~
2 think
3 know
4 drink
5 see
6 sleep
7 buy
8 wear

d	n	k	n	e	w	s
i	s	e	s	b	p	l
d	a	c	w	o	r	e
b	w	m	l	u	k	p
t	h	o	u	g	h	t
a	s	d	j	h	l	m
o	d	e	a	t	i	u
d	r	a	n	k	s	t

2 Complete the sentences with the correct form of the verb.

Last week …

1 John _went_ (go) to Turkey for a holiday.
2 He _____ (leave) at 8 o'clock in the evening.
3 He _____ (meet) some Turkish people on the plane.
4 His new friends _____ (make) Turkish food for him.
5 They _____ (eat) a lot of fish and vegetables.
6 John _____ (have) a great holiday in Turkey.

3 Read the story on page 47 and complete it with the verbs from the box. Use the Past Simple.

~~be~~   wear   see   have   think   sleep
buy   go   leave   want

4 Read the story again. Tick true (✓) and cross false (✗).

1 Brad decided to go to Paris. ✓
2 He hated French food. ☐
3 The plane to Paris was late. ☐
4 The plane didn't arrive in the morning. ☐
5 The people at the airport were French. ☐
6 Brad wasn't in France. ☐

Brad ¹ _was_ a rich Australian on holiday in New York. One night, he ² _____ to a French restaurant for dinner. He loved it!

The next day, Brad phoned the airport and ³ _____ a ticket to Paris. He wanted to eat a lot of French food!

Four hours later, Brad was on the plane to Paris. The plane wasn't very big but it was very nice. And it ⁴ _____ at the right time – 3 o'clock.

Brad enjoyed the trip. He ⁵ _____ a big lunch and then he ⁶ _____ for an hour. The plane arrived at 6 p.m. Brad ⁷ _____ that it was a very short trip.

The Paris airport was very small – Brad was surprised. People talked to him in English – and they all ⁸ _____ big hats! Then he ⁹ _____ a taxi driver by the door.

Brad ¹⁰ _____ to go to the Eiffel Tower. The taxi driver said: 'Sorry, sir. This isn't Paris, France. It's Paris, Texas!' Brad was in the wrong country! What a surprise!

5 Complete the conversation with the verbs in brackets. Use the Past Simple.

Hugo I ¹ _phoned_ (phone) you last night but you ² _____ (not be) at home.

Kevin No, I ³ _____ (drive) to London with Simon. He ⁴ _____ (have) two tickets for a concert.

Hugo What? The Summer Chillfest? I ⁵ _____ (want) to go to that!

Kevin Well, don't worry. It ⁶ _____ (be) terrible. And the tickets ⁷ _____ (cost) €40 each!

Hugo Wow – that was expensive! I ⁸ _____ (see) our favourite local band in the park – and I ⁹ _____ (not pay). It was free!

Kevin The Dakota Dogs? You didn't!

Hugo Yes, I did – they were fantastic! They ¹⁰ _____ (play) all their best songs. And I ¹¹ _____ (meet) Fiona there …

Kevin Fiona!

Hugo Yes, and then we ¹² _____ (go) for a pizza and …

Kevin No! I hate you, Hugo!

6 Correct the underlined phrases.

1 She cooked dinner <u>yesterday night</u>.
  She cooked dinner last night .

2 I listened to music <u>yesterday in the evening</u>.
  _____ .

3 <u>The last Saturday night</u> we watched TV.
  _____ .

4 <u>On last Sunday</u> we walked in the park.
  _____ .

5 <u>At the last weekend</u>, they visited relatives.
  _____ .

6 She phoned her boyfriend <u>today in the morning</u>.
  _____ .

7 Puzzle Write the past tenses in the table and find the Mystery Tour city. You have one minute!

1. meet — M E T
2. see
3. drink
4. wear
5. do
6. make

VOCABULARY

Travel

1 Circle the correct word.

1 He made a solo trip from Gibraltar to Antigua (by)/ *on* boat.
2 They sometimes *bicycle / cycled* to school in the winter.
3 When I was young, I often travelled *by / in* tram.
4 We usually went to work *on / by* foot.
5 They *drove / drives* two thousand kilometres in three days.
6 She travelled a lot in her job and *flies / flew* all over the world.

Prepositions

2 Complete the gaps with the prepositions from the box.

<del>to</del>   by   with   for (x 3)   on   in

Last summer, I went ¹ _to_ the seaside ² _____ my friends. We can't drive so we decided to go ³ _____ train. It was a long journey and we travelled ⁴ _____ five hours. We stayed ⁵ _____ a cheap hotel ⁶ _____ a week. We walked ⁷ _____ the beach every day and ate a lot of fish and chips! We had a great time and wanted to stay ⁸ _____ two weeks!

LISTENING

1 **CD T38** Listen to the phone call. Tick (✓) true and cross (✗) false.

1 Maggie phoned Tania last week. ✓
2 Tania went to Edinburgh by train. ☐
3 She went to the mountains with her friends. ☐
4 They were in the mountains for five days. ☐
5 They really liked Scottish food. ☐
6 They went to clubs every night. ☐

2 **CD T38** Correct the false sentences. Then listen and check.

PRONUNCIATION

/aʊ/ /ɔː/

1 **CD T39** Say the words. Then listen and check.

1 /aʊ/
/saʊθ/ s<u>ou</u>th
/braʊn/ br<u>ow</u>n

2 /ɔː/
/ɔːtəm/ <u>au</u>tumn
/tɔːk/ t<u>a</u>lk

2 **CD T40** Say the words. Then put them in the correct column. Listen and check.

~~proud~~   p<u>o</u>rtable   rec<u>o</u>rd   h<u>ow</u>   A<u>u</u>gust
fl<u>ow</u>er   b<u>o</u>rn   m<u>ou</u>ntain   f<u>ou</u>rth   cl<u>ou</u>d

/aʊ/	/ɔː/
proud	

SURVIVAL ENGLISH

Buying tickets

1 Complete the conversations with the words from the boxes.

One

~~single~~   travel   afternoon   when

A A ¹<u>single</u> to Liverpool, please.
B OK. ² _____ do you want to ³ _____ ?
A This ⁴ _____ before 5 o'clock.
B That's £15, please.

Two

on   back   travel   returns   Friday   when

A Two student ⁵ _____ to London, please.
B OK. And ⁶ _____ do you want to ⁷ _____ ?
A ⁸ _____ Monday. We're coming ⁹ _____ on ¹⁰ _____ night.
B That's £35, please.

2 Read the information below. Then write the conversation.

You are buying a ticket in Oxford. You have to be in Cardiff before 6 p.m. on Saturday. You are coming back on Sunday.

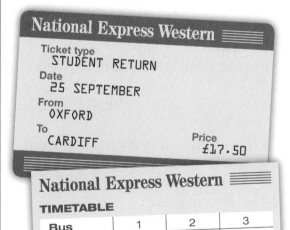

You   <u>A student return to …</u>
Man   _____

49

READING AND WRITING

My Birthday Trip!

Last Saturday was my 18th birthday and I went to London with my friends, Harry and Lola. We drove there in Harry's dad's car and arrived at about 11. Then we started walking. It was Lola's first visit to London so we walked to the Houses of Parliament and saw Big Ben. Then we went on the London Eye – fantastic views of London! After that, we had lunch and relaxed a bit. Then we went to Oxford Street with its famous shops. This time, we went by bus! We stayed there for three hours and I bought a new MP3 player. After that, we drove home. A great birthday!

1 Read the text. Circle the correct answer, a, b or c.

1 Amelia went to London with ___ .
   a friend   **b** two friends   c three friends
2 They went in ___ car.
   a her father's   b Harry's   c Harry's father's
3 ___ knew London.
   a Lola   b They all   c Harry and Amelia
4 They went around London ___ .
   a by bus   b on foot and by bus   c by car
5 They went shopping ___ .
   a in the afternoon   b before lunch
   c for two hours
6 Amelia bought ___ on her birthday.
   a some clothes   b a music player
   c some books

2 Read the box and complete the sentences.

> We use *then* and *after that* to talk about the order of actions. We don't use a comma after *then*.
>
> 1 I got up and had a shower. _____ I had breakfast.
> 2 _____ , I went to school.

3 Underline examples of *then* and *after that* in the text above.

4 Complete the text with *then* or *after that*.

I had a great day yesterday. I went to Oxford by bus with my friend Eddie. We arrived at 10.30 and had a coffee. ¹<u>Then</u> we walked around Oxford for two hours and saw the old universities. ²_____ , we had lunch in a lovely old café. But ³_____ I had a big surprise! Eddie had two tickets to see my favourite football team, Oxford – and they won 2–0! The match finished at 5.30. ⁴_____ , we had a sandwich and went home.

5 Write about a day trip. Use the prompts to help you.

where?	I went to …
when?	on …/ last …/ in …
who with?	I went with …
how?	travelled by ….
what?	walked … / saw … / watched … Then … / After that, …

50

SELF-ASSESSMENT TEST 5 | UNITS 9–10

1 Put the words from the box in the correct column. (5 points)

~~grey~~ March winter gold video red autumn June summer radio spring record pink April yellow camera

Colours	Seasons	Months	Technology
grey			

2 Write the dates. (5 points)

1 5/05/2007
   the fifth of May, two thousand and seven

2 12/08/1998

3 3/01/1964

4 8/02/1645

5 31/11/1815

6 22/09/2008

3 Correct two mistakes in each sentence. (5 points)

1 He leaved on yesterday morning.
   He left yesterday morning .

2 They dranked a lot of cola at last night.

3 She sleeped for twelve hours in Sunday.

4 I went there in bus but I returned by foot.

5 We talk on the phone on last Saturday evening.

6 They sail to New York in the 12th of March 2007.

4 Complete the sentences with the verbs from the box. Use the Past Simple. (5 points)

~~be~~ open go meet make see eat buy

1 It _was_ my birthday last Saturday.
2 My mum _____ breakfast and I _____ a lot!
3 After breakfast, I _____ my presents.
4 Then I _____ shopping and _____ some CDs.
5 At 1 o'clock, I _____ some friends for lunch.
6 After lunch, we _____ a new film at the cinema.

5 Write questions 1–6. Then match them to answers a–f. (10 points)

1 How old / you / 1999?
   How old were you in 1999?   [c]

2 Where / you / born?   [ ]

3 Where / your parents / born? [ ]

4 What / your father's job / when you / primary school? [ ]

5 your mother / teacher?   [ ]

6 Who / your best friend / when you / ten? [ ]

a He worked in a bank.
b His name was Ergun.
c ~~I was ten.~~
d No, she stayed at home. She was a housewife.
e In Istanbul.
f They were born in Antalya, in the south of Turkey.

Total ☐ /30

I know	Yes	No	?
Past Simple of			
• to be all forms: was/wasn't/were/weren't/was he?/were you?	☐	☐	☐
• regular verbs with -ed endings: finished, travelled, wanted	☐	☐	☐
• irregular verbs: went, bought, slept, drove	☐	☐	☐

Childhood

GRAMMAR AND READING

Past Simple: *didn't*

1 Complete the sentences with the negative forms of the underlined verbs.

1 I <u>went</u> to primary school when I was five.
   I <u>didn't go</u> to nursery school.
2 She <u>wanted</u> to be a dancer when she was six.
   She _____ to be a singer.
3 We <u>met</u> our friends in a café after work.
   We _____ them in the street.
4 They <u>ate</u> two pizzas for dinner last night.
   They _____ chicken and vegetables.
5 My mother <u>learnt</u> to drive when she was fifty.
   She _____ to use a computer.
6 I <u>taught</u> my brother to speak English.
   I _____ him to play the piano.

Past Simple

2 Read the table. Then complete the sentences.

	Kelly	Darren
enjoy secondary school	✓	✗
like Maths	✗	✓
study hard	✓	✓
have a lot of friends	✓	✓
go to university	✓	✗
start work	✗	✓

1 Kelly <u>enjoyed</u> secondary school but she <u>didn't like</u> Maths.
2 Darren _____ secondary school but he _____ Maths.
3 Kelly and Darren _____ hard and they _____ a lot of friends.
4 Darren _____ to university after secondary school.
5 He _____ work when he was eighteen.
6 Kelly _____ work when she was eighteen because she _____ to university.

3 Complete the text with the correct verb in the Past Simple.

My mum and dad are musicians and I ¹<u>loved</u> (love) music when I was a kid. I ²_____ (sing) before I ³_____ (start) to talk! My parents ⁴_____ (teach) me to play the piano and the guitar when I was about six, and later I ⁵_____ (learn) the violin. I ⁶_____ (listen) to music all the time on my cassette player – even in bed! But I ⁷_____ (not enjoy) school very much – only music lessons! I ⁸_____ (not like) sports or Maths – but I ⁹_____ (have) a lot of friends. When I was fourteen, we ¹⁰_____ (decide) to start a band, High School Rock. We ¹¹_____ (play) in local clubs and we ¹²_____ (be) very popular. Now we have a record in the Top Ten …

Vocabulary: school

4 Complete the sentences with words from the box.

<s>exams</s>   primary   university   nursery   secondary   classes

1 Her daughter passed all her A-level <u>exams</u> last week.
2 She finished _____ and started work last July.
3 They went to a great _____ school when they were eleven.
4 My dad goes to French _____ after work on Wednesday.
5 When I was six, my favourite _____ school teacher was Mrs Jones.
6 Their son started _____ school when he was three.

GRAMMAR AND SPEAKING

Past Simple questions

Last Saturday …

1. Write questions and answers about Jason.

   1. get up early?
      Did he get up early?
      No, he didn't. He got
      up late.

   2. phone his mother?
      _____
      _____
      _____
      _____

   3. go swimming?
      _____
      _____
      _____
      _____

   4. eat a hamburger?
      _____
      _____
      _____
      _____

   5. see a football match?
      _____
      _____
      _____
      _____

   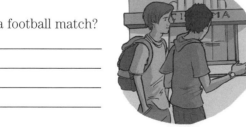

   6. read a magazine?
      _____
      _____
      _____
      _____

2. Write questions and answers about *you*.

   1. When _did you start_ (start) school?
      I started school when I was six.
   2. What TV programmes _____ (enjoy) when you were a child?
      _____.
   3. What _____ (be) your favourite toy?
      _____.
   4. What music _____ (listen to)?
      _____.
   5. What food _____ (like) to eat?
      _____.
   6. What _____ (do) in your free time?
      _____.

Vocabulary: word groups

3. Circle the odd one out.

   1. boat   train   [robot]
   2. books   magazines   cartoons
   3. terrible   cool   boring
   4. pyjamas   suit   uniform
   5. videos   toys   DVDs
   6. teenager   kid   child

4. Complete the sentences with the circled words from Exercise 1.

   1. My mum wants a _robot_ for Christmas – to cook for her!
   2. It was great to be a _____ in the 1990s.
   3. We didn't watch _____ when we were kids. We didn't have a TV!
   4. It was _____ to have a glossy black mobile in 2007.
   5. The children played with their _____ all afternoon.
   6. I'm twenty-one and I still wear my *Simpsons* _____ to bed!

VOCABULARY

School

1 Put your favourite subjects in order, 1–6.

Art ☐ History ☐
Maths ☐ Geography ☐
Biology ☐ Chemistry ☐

2 Complete words 1–10. Then match them to the correct pictures.

1 k e y s [b]
2 _ _ c _ _ _ c _ ☐
3 _ _ _ _ _ o o _ ☐
4 _ a _ t _ _ ☐
5 _ e _ c _ _ ☐
6 _ _ l _ _ _ a _ _ r ☐
7 _ e _ _ ☐
8 _ a _ _ _ ☐
9 c _ _ f _ e m _ _ ☐
10 _ e _ ☐

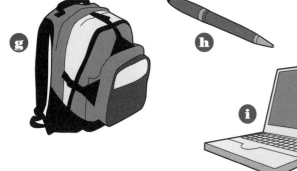

3 Complete the sentences with the correct nouns.

1 *Friends* was my favourite TV _programme_ when I was young.
2 Her daughter wants to study _____ Technology at university.
3 It's Harry's coffee _____ . It has his name on it.
4 I went to see my Geography teacher in the _____ room.
5 I worked in a supermarket in my last _____ holidays.
6 Our _____ Education teacher played football for Wales in 2001.

4 Match verbs 1–6 with words a–f.

1 start [d]   a a lot of friends
2 study ☐   b famous
3 have ☐   c History
4 be ☐   d university
5 go back ☐ e doing exercises
6 enjoy ☐   f home

5 Puzzle Read the clues and write the answers in the puzzle. Then complete the word in the grey boxes. Clue: it's the opposite of *easy*!

❶ A book with words and their meanings.
❷ A modern technology subject.
❸ A top job in a university.
❹ They talk and drink coffee in the staff room.
❺ A language and a school subject.
❻ The story of the past.

1 D I C T I O N A R Y
2 ☐☐☐☐☐☐☐☐☐☐
3 ☐☐☐☐☐☐☐☐☐
4 ☐☐☐☐☐☐☐
5 ☐☐☐☐☐☐
6 ☐☐☐☐☐☐☐

PRONUNCIATION

/ʊ/ /uː/ /juː/

1 [CD T41] Say the words. Then listen and repeat.

1 /ʊ/
/gʊd/ g<u>oo</u>d
/ˈtekstbʊk/ textb<u>oo</u>k

2 /uː/
/fuːd/ f<u>oo</u>d
/kɑːˈtuːn/ cart<u>oo</u>n

3 /juː/
/ˈpjuːpəl/ p<u>u</u>pil
/ʌnˈjuːʒuəl/ un<u>u</u>sual

2 [CD T42] Say the words in the box and put them in the correct column. Then listen and check.

<u>school</u> childh<u>oo</u>d T<u>ue</u>sday sh<u>oe</u> c<u>oo</u>k <u>u</u>niversity f<u>oo</u>tball J<u>u</u>ly b<u>oo</u>t comp<u>u</u>ter classr<u>oo</u>m <u>u</u>sually

/ʊ/	/uː/	/juː/
	school	

SURVIVAL ENGLISH

Small talk

1 Match sentences 1–3 with pictures A–C.

1 Terrible weather today. ☐
2 I love your hat! ☐
3 I studied all night. I feel terrible. ☐

A Thank you. It was very expensive.

B Did you have a nice evening?

C Yes, it's awful.

2 Complete the coversations with the words from the box.

<s>have</s> Lovely interesting school It's childhood this weather Did Thanks holiday bag

1 A Did you ¹<u>have</u> a nice ² _____ ?
   B Not really. The ³ _____ was terrible.

2 A Your ⁴ _____ 's really great.
   B ⁵ _____ . I bought it in Spain.

3 A How's ⁶ _____ , Milly?
   B ⁷ _____ OK, thanks, granddad.

4 A Nice weather ⁸ _____ morning.
   B Yes, it is. ⁹ _____ .

5 A ¹⁰ _____ you see that TV programme about ¹¹ _____ ?
   B Yes. It was very ¹² _____ .

12 Shopping

GRAMMAR AND SPEAKING

Vocabulary

1 Circle the correct word.

1 I like *casual* / *relaxed* clothes.
2 How much did that book *cost* / *buy*?
3 We really enjoyed our shopping *trip* / *journey* yesterday.
4 He went to the cinema *single* / *alone* last night.
5 I love walking on the *beach* / *seaside*.
6 She went on holiday *with* / *by* her family

Questions: all tenses

2 Circle the correct answer, a, b or c.

1 What ___ do last weekend?
  a do you   b are you   **c** did you
2 Where ___ last Saturday afternoon?
  a he was   b you were   c were you
3 When ___ buy a car?
  a he did   b did he   c does he
4 Who ___ to now?
  a is she talking   b does she talk   c she talks
5 How ___ home yesterday?
  a do they get   b they got   c did they get
6 Why ___ work today? It's Sunday.
  a I have to   b do I have to   c I have to

Question words

3 Match the question words 1–8 to answers a–h.

1 What?   c
2 Why?   □
3 How?   □
4 When?   □
5 Where? □
6 Who?   □
7 How much? □
8 What time? □

a On Saturday evening.
b By train.
~~c Two CDs and a book.~~
d On the Internet.
e Belinda.
f At ten to five.
g Because I love this music.
h €15 for three.

Wh- questions

4 Write the questions. Then match them to answers a–h in Exercise 3.

1 buy / in / did / town / What / today? / you
  What did you buy in town today?   c
2 buy / you / your / Where / usually / clothes? / do
  _____ □
3 time / does / What / bookshop / open? / the
  _____ □
4 they / to / How / get / do / work?
  _____ □
5 much / those / How / T-shirts? / were
  _____ □
6 Andrea? / see / did / When / he
  _____ □
7 you / CDs? / have to / buy / Why / do / three
  _____ □
8 the / Who / at / party? / did / Peter / to / talk
  _____ □

Why? questions

5 Write *Why?* questions in the correct tense. Then match them with answers a–e.

1 she / tired / this morning?
  Why was she tired this morning?   b
2 you / angry / with me / yesterday?
  _____ □
3 your mum / have to / go to shops / now?
  _____ □
4 the students / happy / today?
  _____ □
5 Mark / go to bed / at 9 / last night?
  _____ □

a Because he was very tired.
~~b Because she studied all night.~~
c Because they passed their exams.
d Because you didn't phone me!
e Because she has to buy some food.

GRAMMAR AND VOCABULARY

Clothes

1 Find nine more clothes words in the box. Look → and ↓.

e	t	j	a	c	k	e	t	u	i
t	c	b	n	s	k	i	r	t	t
r	a	c	x	w	m	o	p	l	r
a	d	a	j	e	a	n	s	m	o
i	v	p	u	a	w	a	h	n	u
n	s	u	i	t	h	s	o	b	s
e	v	l	y	e	g	d	e	p	e
r	d	p	e	r	t	f	s	h	r
s	a	s	h	i	r	t	t	r	s

this/that, these/those

2 Complete the questions and answers.

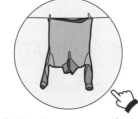

1 What's <u>this</u> ?
   It's a _____ .

2 What's _____ ?
   It's a _____ .

3 What are _____ ?
   They're _____ .

4 What _____ ?
   _____ _____ .

3 Write the sentences in the plural.

1 That green sweater is nice.
   <u>Those green sweaters are nice</u> .

2 That grey suit is very expensive.
   _____ .

3 How much is this blue shirt?
   _____ .

4 Look at that lovely yellow cap!
   _____ .

5 That red skirt looks awful.
   _____ .

6 I bought this black jacket last year.
   _____ .

4 Read the sentences. Match them to the right people. Then complete the sentences with *this*, *that*, *these* or *those*.

a I have to buy <u>these</u> lovely flowers!   [1]
b _____ shoes look really smart.   [ ]

c _____ chocolate cake looks good.   [ ]
d I quite like _____ coffee.   [ ]

e _____ bag is very expensive.   [ ]
f _____ hats are great.   [ ]

57

VOCABULARY AND LISTENING

Vocabulary: clothes

1 Match the words from the box to 1–9 in photo A.

tights [8]
glasses [ ]
tie [ ]
hat [ ]
shirt [ ]
jacket [ ]
glove [ ]
boot [ ]

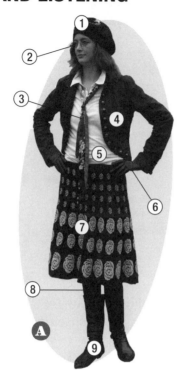

2 Complete the sentences about photo A.

1 _She isn't wearing_ trousers.
2 _____ cap.
3 _____ gloves.
4 _____ a shirt.
5 _____ a dress.
6 _____ socks.

3 Write true sentences about photo B. Use the words from the box.

~~cap~~ trainers watch trousers socks
T-shirt

1 _She isn't wearing_ a hat.
  She's wearing a cap .
2 _____
  a shirt and tie.
  _____ .
3 _____
  gloves.
  _____ .
4 _____
  skirt.
  _____ .
5 _____
  boots.
  _____ .
6 _____
  tights.
  _____ .

LISTENING

1 [CD T43] Listen and circle the correct answer, a or b.

1 Josh ___ his father's birthday.
  a remembered **b** didn't remember
2 Their father's birthday is ___ .
  a on Friday 5th July b next Thursday
3 Mel ___ what present to buy for their father.
  a knows b doesn't know
4 They ___ their father books for his last birthday.
  a gave b didn't give
5 Their father ___ listens to classical music.
  a never b sometimes
6 ___ things on the Internet.
  a Josh buys b Josh's friends buy
7 They decide to buy their father ___ .
  a a T-shirt b a sweater
8 Josh ___ how to use the Internet.
  a knows b doesn't know

PRONUNCIATION

Sounds revision

1 [CD T44] Complete the table with the words from the box. Then listen and check.

~~dress~~ glasses tights socks boots
cap shirt gloves trousers trainers

/e/	/eɪ/	/ɑː/	/æ/	/aɪ/
sw**ea**ter	p**ay**	sm**ar**t	j**a**cket	t**ie**
dress				

/ɒ/	/ɜː/	/aʊ/	/ʌ/	/uː/
w**a**tch	sk**ir**t	s**ou**nd	m**u**g	sh**oe**s

2 [CD T45] Write the questions. Then listen and check.

1 /weə/ /də/ /ju/ /ˈjuːʒəli/ /ɡəʊ/ /ˈʃɒpɪŋ/ ?
  Where do you usually go shopping ?
2 /waɪ/ /də/ /ju/ /ɡəʊ/ /ðeə/ ?
  _____ ?
3 /wɒt/ /wəz/ /ðə/ /lɑːst/ /θɪŋ/ /ju/ /bɔːt/ ?
  _____ ?
4 /haʊ/ /mʌtʃ/ /dɪd/ /ɪt/ /kɒst/ ?
  _____ ?

SURVIVAL ENGLISH

In a shop

1 **CD T46** Listen and match the conversations to pictures A–C.

1 ☐   2 ☐   3 ☐

2 **CD T46** Complete the conversations with one word in each gap. Then listen and check.

1 **Man** ¹<u>Excuse</u> me. Do you have these ²_____ in an ³_____ large, please?

Shop assistant I'm sorry, sir. We only ⁴_____ them in medium and large.

2 **Polly** It ⁵_____ lovely, Jess. Does it ⁶_____?

Jess I'm not sure. It's a ⁷_____ short.

Polly No, it ⁸_____ perfect!

3 **Woman** Can I ⁹_____ on those boots, please?

Shop assistant Yes, of course. What ¹⁰_____?

Woman Black, please.

3 Put the conversation in the correct order.

Shop assistant
Yes, we do. What size are you? ☐
Here you are. ☐
Can I help you, sir? ☐ 1
Yes, of course. The changing rooms are over there. ☐
It's in the sale. It's now €70. ☐

Customer
Thank you very much. ☐
And do you have it in grey? ☐
Oh, that looks nice. Can I try it on? ☐
Yes. How much is that suit, please? ☐
I think I'm a large. ☐

4 Write a conversation in a shop. Use the information below.

A brown jacket.
Size: large
Price: €40

A <u>Excuse me. Do you have …</u>_____?
B _____?

READING AND WRITING

School uniforms – past and present

A In the past, all pupils at English schools wore a uniform. They were all the same style and were usually quite ugly. It wasn't so bad for the boys. They usually wore a shirt and tie, trousers, a jacket (called a *blazer*), and socks and shoes. They also wore caps, and the young boys wore short trousers. But the uniforms for girls were awful! They wore skirts but they *also* wore a shirt and tie – and a blazer, hat, and socks and shoes. That was the winter uniform. In the summer, they happily changed to dresses. They were all the same colour and style – but no shirts or ties. They loved the summer!

B many schoolchildren in england don't have to wear uniforms now in some schools parents and children can decide if they want to wear a uniform or not some pupils do and others don't at my school the girls sometimes wear trousers they don't have to wear skirts we wear jeans and t-shirts in the summer but the jeans have to be black and the t-shirts have to be white in the winter we wear blue sweaters we also have to wear black shoes not trainers to school i like it its a uniform but a nice uniform

1 Read text A and answer the questions.

1 What did all English pupils wear in the past?
   <u>They all wore a uniform</u>.
2 Were they nice uniforms? Why/Why not?
   _____.
3 What did young boys wear?
   _____.
4 Why were the uniforms for girls awful?
   _____.
5 Why did they love the summer?
   _____.

2 Look at text B. What's wrong with it?

3 Read the box and match 1–4 with a–d.

Sentences
1 A **sentence** usually has [b]
2 We use a **capital letter** [ ]
3 We use a **full stop** (.) [ ]
4 We link sentences with [ ]
a to finish a sentence.
b a subject, verb and object.
c *and, but, then*.
d to start a sentence.

4 Tick (✓) the sentences that *are* sentences!

1 I live in   [ ]
2 She loves clothes. [ ]
3 Is on the Internet. [ ]
4 At 10 o'clock.   [ ]
5 They bought it in. [ ]
6 He watched TV.   [ ]

5 Rewrite text B. Use capital letters, full stops, apostrophes and commas.

Many schoolchildren in England don't have to wear uniforms now.

6 Write about school uniforms in your country in the past and now.

In the past, schoolchildren in my country wore …

60

SELF-ASSESSMENT TEST 6 | UNITS 11–12

1 Complete the school subjects. (5 points)

1 B i o l o g y
2 _ e _ _ _ a _ _ _
3 _ i _ _ _ _ y
4 _ _ _ _ i _ _ r _
5 _ _ t _ _ _ a _ i _ _
6 _ n _ _ _ _ h

2 Complete the crossword. (5 points)

```
  2 B L A C K B O A R 3 D
      4     C     5
      6     7     T
            8     T     9
      C                 E
                  10
            11          L
```

ACROSS ▶
2 The teacher uses it a lot!
4 A bag
7 A portable computer
8 You're using it now!
11 A school student

DOWN ▼
1 We use it for Maths.
3 You have them in your classroom.
5 You use colours in this subject.
6 We can write with this.
9 People have these for their car, house …
10 We drink from this.

3 Circle the correct answer, a or b. (5 points)

1 He bought a new ___ but he doesn't like it.
   a trousers   **b** jacket
2 Can I try on this ___ , please?
   a trainers   b skirt
3 Where did you buy that ___ ?
   a hat   b socks
4 It's cold today. Wear a hat and ___ .
   a tie   b gloves
5 Do you have any ___ in extra small?
   a shirt   b tights
6 Does the red ___ fit?
   a dress   b caps

4 Circle the correct word. (5 points)

1 Is **this** / these your rucksack?
2 Where did you buy those / this jeans?
3 Why does he listen to that / these loud music?
4 Can you give me these / those pens, please?
5 What are those / that kids doing?
6 This / That exercise is very easy!

5 Tick (✓) the correct sentence, a or b. (5 points)

1 a I didn't started school when I was five. ☐
  b I didn't start school when I was five. ✓
2 a We don't want to go out last night. ☐
  b We didn't want to go out last night. ☐
3 a Did they ate my chocolate cake? ☐
  b Did they eat my chocolate cake? ☐
4 a Maxine didn't felt very well yesterday. ☐
  b Maxine didn't feel very well yesterday. ☐
5 a You did understand the question? ☐
  b Did you understand the question? ☐
6 a He didn't drive fast when he was young. ☐
  b He doesn't drive fast when he was young. ☐

6 Complete the questions. (5 points)

1 _Where did you buy_ that rucksack?
  I bought it on the Internet.
2 _____ at university?
  They studied History.
3 _____ to Spain?
  We go there every year.
4 _____ their last shopping trip?
  It was last month.
5 _____ her boyfriend for Christmas?
  She gave him a CD.
6 _____ to the shopping centre?
  No, not very often. I go there once a month.

Total ☐ /30

I know	Yes	No	?
• Past Simple: negative and questions *didn't study, did you go?*	☐	☐	☐
• Question words: *what, when, why, where, how, how much*	☐	☐	☐
• Question forms in the present and past tenses	☐	☐	☐
• *this, that, these, those*	☐	☐	☐

61

SELF-ASSESSMENT TESTS: ANSWER KEY

TEST 1 | UNITS 1–2

1 **Countries** Canada, Germany
   Nationalities French, American, Italian
2 2 56 3 15 4 33 5 25 6 100
   7 12 8 40 9 94 10 8 11 67
3 2 a writer 3 a secretary 4 an engineer 5 a mechanic
   6 a receptionist
4 2a 3b 4a 5b 6a
5 2 Anna's a police officer.
   3 She's Polish.
   4 Adam's an electrician.
   5 Her name's Helen.
   6 She's from Russia.
6 2 Mr Kelly isn't an actor.
   3 I'm not/am not an engineer.
   4 Is Mrs Thomas your teacher?
   5 Tim is a mechanic from Ireland.
   6 You aren't/are not from France.

TEST 2 | UNITS 3–4

1 (Possible answers)
   Family mother, father, son, parents, sister, brother, aunt, uncle, grandmother, etc.
   Places hotel, park, café, bank, library, museum, church, etc.
2 2 interesting 3 short 4 new 5 terrible 6 rich
3 2b 3a 4a 5b 6b
4 2 Her uncle's wife is from New York.
   3 Her husband's father is a teacher.
   4 Carol's daughter is very pretty.
   5 Jack's girlfriend is Spanish.
   6 Their sister's son is a student.
5 2 There aren't any supermarkets in the town.
   3 They aren't engineers.
   4 There isn't a cinema here.
   5 We aren't from Ireland.
   6 There aren't any shoe shops near here.
6 2 Are their grandparents from here? d
   3 How many churches are there in Bath? f
   4 Are there any good clothes shops near here? e
   5 Is there an internet café in the town centre? a
   6 Where are the toilets, please? b

TEST 3 | UNITS 5–6

1 **Food and drink** chicken, milk, cheese, eggs, tea
   Music and free time hip hop, jazz, films, books, basketball
   Days and times of the day Monday, Thursday, evening, Tuesday, afternoon
2 2 twenty past two
   3 twenty-five past three
   4 quarter to eight
   5 five to twelve
3 2 at; on 3 at; in 4 to; on 5 to; on 6 at; at
4 2 usually 3 never 4 usually 5 never 6 sometimes
5 2 eats it 3 like them 4 eat it 5 speaks it 6 like me
6 2 Where do Suzy and George live; They live
   3 Do your grandparents speak Polish; they don't
   4 Does your brother like jazz; he doesn't. He likes
   5 What languages do you and your sister speak; We speak
   6 Does Annie play basketball; does

TEST 4 | UNITS 7–8

1 **Across** 3 chair 4 table 5 bed
   Down 2 fridge 3 cooker
2 2 shower 3 badly 4 drive 5 cook 6 guitarist
3 (Possible answers)
   2 a book/an email
   3 loudly/fast
   4 a sandwich/lunch/dinner
   5 the radio
   6 a film/DVD
   7 the newspaper/a magazine
   8 a suit/a shirt
   9 relatives
   10 mum/dad
   11 slowly/hard
4 2 Do; have to do
   3 can't speak
   4 have to be
   5 Can; dance
   6 don't have to cook
5 2 They can't play football.
   3 Do you want to go to the cinema?
   4 Are they surfing the Internet again?
   5 I have to study for a test now.
   6 Do you play the violin at school?
6 2 Is she learning English at school? f
   3 Are they walking the dog? a
   4 When do you have to go? b
   5 Where are they playing tonight? e
   6 What do you have to do this evening? d

TEST 5 | UNITS 9–10

1 **Colours** gold, red, pink, yellow
   Seasons winter, autumn, summer, spring
   Months March, June, April
   Technology video, radio, record, camera
2 2 the twelfth of August, nineteen ninety-eight
   3 the third of January, nineteen sixty-four
   4 the eighth of February, sixteen forty-five
   5 the thirty-first of November, eighteen fifteen
   6 the twenty-second of September, two thousand and eight
3 2 They drank a lot of cola last night.
   3 She slept for twelve hours on Sunday.
   4 I went there by bus but I returned on foot.
   5 We talked on the phone last Saturday evening.
   6 They sailed to New York on the 12th of March 2007.
4 2 made; ate 3 opened 4 went; bought 5 met 6 saw
5 2 Where were you born? e
   3 Where were your parents born? f
   4 What was your father's job when you were at primary school? a
   5 Was your mother a teacher? d
   6 Who was your best friend when you were ten? b

TEST 6 | UNITS 11–12

1 2 Geography 3 History 4 Chemistry 5 Mathematics
   6 English
2 **Across** 4 rucksack 7 laptop 8 textbook 11 pupil
   Down 1 calculator 3 desks 5 art 6 pencil 9 keys 10 mug
3 2b 3a 4b 5b 6a
4 2 those 3 that 4 those 5 those 6 This
5 2b 3b 4b 5b 6a
6 2 What did they study
   3 How often do you go
   4 When was
   5 What did she give
   6 How often do you go

WORKBOOK TAPESCRIPT

UNIT 1 Hi!

Track 2. Grammar and vocabulary, Exercise 2

1
Dave   Hello. I'm Dave.
Amélie Hi, Dave. My name's Amélie. Where are you from?
Dave   I'm from Canada. And where are you from?
Amélie I'm from Paris. I'm French.

2
Silvia Hi. My name's Silvia.
Karl   Hello. I'm Karl. Where are you from?
Silvia I'm from Italy. And you?
Karl   I'm German. I'm from Berlin.

3
Jane   Hello. I'm Jane.
Fernando Hi, Jane! My name's Fernando. Where are you from?
Jane   I'm from London. I'm English. And you?
Fernando I'm from Buenos Aires. I'm Argentinian.

Track 3. Vocabulary, Exercise 2

1 three 2 five 3 fifteen 4 fifty
5 thirteen 6 thirty 7 eighty-eight
8 a hundred

Track 4. Vocabulary, Exercise 4

1 I'm fifty and I'm a teacher.
2 I'm fifteen and I'm a student.
3 I'm not twelve. I'm twenty.
4 A How old are you?
  B I'm eighteen.
5 A Sorry? Are you seven?
  B No, I'm eleven!

Track 5. Pronunciation, Exercise 1

1 /e/ ten French
2 /eɪ/ name Spain

Track 6. Pronunciation, Exercise 2

Across Naples, Mexico, twenty
Down   twelve, Canadian, eight

Track 7. Survival English, Exercise 1

1 Ben   Afternoon, Helen!
  Helen Hi, Ben. How are you?
  Ben   Fine, thanks. And you?
  Helen Yes, I'm fine, thanks.
2 John   Good morning, Mrs Smith.
  Mrs Smith Good morning, John. How are you?
  John   I'm very well, thank you. And you?
  Mrs Smith Yes, I'm very well, thank you.

UNIT 2 Jobs

Track 8. Vocabulary, Exercise 1

1 A What's your name?
  B It's Sheila. S-h-e-i-l-a.
2 A Are you German?
  B Yes, I'm from Munich: M-u-n-i-c-h.
3 A Where's Rio de Janeiro?
  B It's in Brazil. B-r-a-z-i-l.
4 A Where's Peter from?
  B He's from Liverpool. L-i-v-e-r-p-o-o-l.
5 A How old are you?
  B I'm eighteen. E-i-g-h-t-e-e-n.
6 A Is Maria Italian?
  B No, she's Greek. G-r-e-e-k.

Track 9. Pronunciation, Exercise 1

1 /ɑː/ France   artist
2 /æ/ bag Canada

Track 10. Pronunciation, Exercise 2

1 /ɑː/ aren't pardon Martin afternoon
2 /æ/ Italian Dan married Spanish mechanic thanks

Track 11. Survival English, Exercise 1

A Excuse me. Where's HSBC?
B Pardon?
A HSBC.
B HSBC? I'm sorry, I'm from Germany. I don't understand.
A It's a bank.
B Oh, a bank! Sorry, I don't know.

UNIT 3 Family life

Track 12. Listening, Exercise 1

Emily My family isn't very big. My grandmother's name is Elizabeth. Her daughter is my mum, and her son is my uncle Frank. He's married to Lily. Their son Freddy is twenty. We're very good friends.
Lily My husband's mother is from Germany but my husband is English. His sister's name is Grace. Grace's daughter is Emily. She's eighteen. She and my son are students at university.
Freddy My dad's an engineer and my mum's a teacher. She's from Manchester. My dad's sister is a singer and her husband is my uncle Harry. He's a doctor. My grandmother is from Berlin but my parents are English.
Elizabeth My children, Frank and Grace, are married and I'm a grandmother. Frank wife's name is Lily. She's a teacher and their son's name is Freddy. Grace's husband is a doctor and his name's Harry. Their daughter, Emily is eighteen.

Track 13. Pronunciation, Exercise 1

1 /æ/ dad family
2 /ʌ/ mum uncle

Track 14. Pronunciation, Exercise 2

ugly bag London happy Spanish
husband mother brother actor
Russia bad son

Track 15. Pronunciation, Exercise 3

1 Her mum's from Russia.
2 My uncle's in London.
3 His son's car is ugly.
4 He's a bad actor.
5 My husband's Spanish.
6 Their brother's my dad.

UNIT 4 Places

Track 16. Listening, Exercise 1

Hi, I'm Jerry and I'm nineteen. My parents are teachers here in New York City. They're from Italy but I'm American. I'm a student at Columbia University here. New York's a great place! It's very big and there are a lot of interesting things to do. The university is near Times Square. There are over fifty theatres and cinemas there – and some great clubs, too. The New York museums are fantastic! And there are some very good cafés and restaurants – American, French, and a lot of great Italian restaurants too, of course! New York isn't boring. There's only one small problem: there are a lot of people, cars and buses in the streets. It's terrible.

Track 17. Pronunciation, Exercise 1

1 /ɒ/ shop on
2 /əʊ/ hotel no

Track 18. Pronunciation, Exercise 2

1 /ɒ/ job office sorry opposite hospital
2 /əʊ/ clothes post only don't know

UNIT 5 Likes and dislikes

Track 19. Pronunciation. Exercise 1

1 /ʃ/ fish she
2 /tʃ/ chips cheese
3 /dʒ/ orange juice

Track 20. Pronunciation, Exercise 2

1 shoe 2 shop 3 language
4 Turkish 5 church 6 German
7 chicken 8 vegetables 9 receptionist
10 sandwich 11 engineer 12 chocolate

Track 21. Survival English, Exercise 1

1 one pound sixty
2 fifty-four p
3 three pounds fifty-five
4 eight pounds ninety-nine
5 eighteen p
6 twenty-six pounds eighty-nine
7 fifteen pounds fifty
8 twelve pounds thirty

Track 22. Survival English, Exercise 3

Girl   A chicken sandwich and a chocolate cake, please.
Young man Sure. Anything else?
Girl   Yes. A coffee, please.
Young man Right … Here you are.
Girl   How much is that?
Young man Um, a coffee … that's one pound ten; a chicken sandwich, two pounds twenty. That's um, three pounds thirty … and a chocolate cake – one pound fifty … um, that's five pounds eighty … um, no, sorry, four pounds eighty … , please.
Girl   Four pounds eighty … Oh sorry! How much is a fruit juice?
Young man Ummm … it's one pound sixty.
Girl   Oh. OK, a mineral water then, please.
Young man A mineral water … Here you are. Um, it's seventy-five p … so four pounds eighty and seventy-five … that's, um … five pounds …
Girl   Five pounds fifty-five!
Young man Thank you! Yes … five pounds fifty-five.

UNIT 6 Routines

Track 23. Listening, Exercise 1

Will   Here's your coffee
Isabel Thanks, Will.
Will   Where do you come from, Isabel?
Isabel Mendoza. It's a big city in Argentina.
Will   Argentina? Great! And do you like England?
Isabel Yes, I love it. But it's very different.
Will   Really? How?

Isabel	Well, you do things at different times here in England! You eat and sleep at different times.
Will	Do we? When do you eat and sleep in Mendoza then?
Isabel	Well, you see, shops close at 2 o'clock – so people don't usually work in the afternoon.
Will	Oh! So what do they do in the afternoon?
Isabel	They have a big lunch and then they relax. They sometimes have a 'siesta' …
Will	A siesta? They go to bed? That's a very good idea! Do you sleep in the afternoons, Isabel?
Isabel	Not in England!
Will	Right!
Isabel	But at home, yes … I sometimes have a siesta – but I usually study.
Will	Do you go to school in the evening, too?
Isabel	No, I don't. I'm at university in Mendoza now. But schools start and finish at different times there. My brother goes to school in the morning – he starts at 8 and finishes at 2. But my sister starts at 2 – and finishes at 8 in the evening.
Will	So she doesn't get up early in the morning!
Isabel	No, never. She loves it!
Will	But she finishes school very late. When does she have dinner?
Isabel	At the normal time … in Argentina! My family usually eats at about 11. We never have dinner at 7 – and we never go to bed early!
Will	Great. I want to live in Mendoza! But 11 is very late to eat …

Track 24. Vocabulary and Speaking, Exercise 3

1. ten past nine
2. twenty to twelve
3. ten past three
4. twenty-five past seven
5. five to two
6. quarter to eleven

Track 25. Pronunciation, Exercise 1

1. /ɜː/ w<u>or</u>k <u>ear</u>ly
2. /ɔː/ f<u>our</u> sp<u>or</u>t

Track 26. Pronunciation, Exercise 2

Across burger, shirt, forty, morning, Saturday
Down quarter, boring, Thursday, thirty

Track 27. Survival English, Exercise 1

1. **A** What time does the bus leave Oxford, please?
   B At ten past two.
   A Thank you.
2. **A** What time does John's train arrive?
   B It arrives at quarter past six.
3. **A** Excuse me. Is there a post office near here?
   B Yes, it's over there, next to the library.
   A When does it close?
   B I think it closes at 1 on Saturday.
4. **A** What's on TV tonight?
   B There's *Friends* at 8. Then there's a film.
   A What time does it start?
   B At 9 o'clock.

UNIT 7 Talent

Track 28. Vocabulary, Exercise 2

1. a group of people laughing
2. car engine sound
3. someone playing/practising the piano quietly and gently
4. Commentator: … and the ball goes to Thierry Henry and – oh! – it's a GOOOOAL!!!
5. Woman: Hello Marco. Is Susan at home?
6. someone playing the violin very badly

Track 29. Listening, Exercise 1

Laura	Are you good at sports, Mark?
Mark	Well, some sports, yes.
Laura	Can you play basketball?
Mark	Yes – but I'm terrible! I'm a good tennis player, I play for my college team.
Laura	Great. I love tennis, too. Can you speak any languages?
Mark	No – only English! But you know that of course – it's because I am English and I can speak it very fast!
Laura	Yes, I know! I know! Please speak slowly!
Mark	OK – sorry Laura! But your English is fantastic!
Laura	Thank you …. And what about music? Can you sing or play any instruments?
Mark	Yes, I love music! I can play the guitar but I don't play it at home – my mum doesn't like loud music! I have to play at a friend's house – we have a rock group. And I can sing a bit – but not very well. I have to sing in the bathroom when I have a shower – and not loudly!
Laura	Right! And do you have a car? Can you drive?
Mark	Well, I don't have a car but I sometimes drive my brother's. It's very old so you can't drive it fast.
Laura	Well, that's great. I don't like fast drivers!

Track 30. Pronunciation, Exercise 1

1. /b/ <u>b</u>ad <u>b</u>ook
2. /v/ <u>v</u>iolin ne<u>v</u>er

UNIT 8 Free time

Track 31. Pronunciation, Exercise 1

1. /w/ <u>w</u>alk sho<u>w</u>er
2. /v/ <u>v</u>isit T<u>V</u>
3. /f/ <u>f</u>unny <u>ph</u>one

Track 32. Pronunciation, Exercise 2

Across water, fridge, laugh, DVD, evening
Down sofa, video, weekend, wear, watch

Track 33. Survival English, Exercise 1

A Do you have any plans for tomorrow afternoon?
B No, I don't. Why?
A There's a concert on at the football stadium. Do you want to go?
B Yes – great!
A OK. Let's meet at 2.30.
B Where?
A In the café near the stadium.
B OK. See you tomorrow.

UNIT 9 Changes

Track 34. Reading and Vocabulary, Exercise 1

1. nineteen eighty-one
2. sixteen fifty-three
3. eighteen eighty
4. two thousand and five
5. nineteen ninety-four
6. two thousand and sixteen

Track 35. Vocabulary and Listening, Exercise 2

1. the twenty-fourth of March
2. the eighteenth of December
3. the eleventh of August
4. the thirty-first of May
5. the third of February
6. the twelfth of September

Track 36. Pronunciation, Exercise 1

1. /wəz/
   Was he at school?
   No, he was at home.
   /wə/
   Were they at home?
   No, they were at school.
2. /wɒz/
   Where was he?
   He wasn't at home.
   /wɜː/
   Where were they?
   They weren't at school.

Track 37. Pronunciation, Exercise 2

1. Was he at home yesterday?
   Was he at home yesterday?
2. Yes, he was.
   Yes, he was.
3. Was he with her last night?
   Was he with her last night?
4. No, he wasn't.
   No, he wasn't.
5. Where were you last night?
   Where were you last night?
6. We were in a club.
   We were in a club.
7. Were you happy?
   Were you happy?
8. Yes, we were.
   Yes, we were.

UNIT 10 Travel

Track 38. Listening, Exercise 1

Maggie	Hi. Tania, where are you?
Tania	Oh hi, Maggie. I'm at home of course!
Maggie	But I phoned you three times last week and you weren't there.
Tania	No, I was on holiday in Scotland! I arrived home this morning.
Maggie	Scotland? Where – Edinburgh?
Tania	No, we flew to Edinburgh – the tickets were very cheap. But then we went to the mountains.
Maggie	The mountains!?
Tania	Yes. I went with my sister and two of her friends. We went there by bus from Edinburgh – it was a long journey – four hours!
Maggie	How long were you there?
Tania	We stayed for five days. We walked every day – the mountains were fantastic! And we stayed in very small hotels and ate amazing Scottish food – a lot of it!
Maggie	But Tania, there aren't any clubs or cinemas in the mountains!
Tania	Yes, we knew that! But we were

SELF-ASSESSMENT TEST 1 | UNITS 1–2

1 Put the words from the box in the correct column. (5 points)

~~Turkey~~   French   American   Canada   Germany   Italian

Countries	Nationalities
Turkey	

2 Match the numbers to the words. (5 points)

25   56   8   40   15   12
33   67   ~~71~~   94   100

1 seventy-one _71_
2 fifty-six ____
3 fifteen ____
4 thirty-three ____
5 twenty-five ____
6 a hundred ____
7 twelve ____
8 forty ____
9 ninety-four ____
10 eight ____
11 sixty-seven ____

3 Complete the jobs. Write *a* or *an*. (5 points)

1 _a_ _s_ _i_ _n_ _g_ _e_ _r_
2 _ w _ _ _ e r
3 _ _ e _ _ _ t _ _ y
4 _ _ _ g _ _ _ e r
5 _ m _ _ _ a _ _ c
6 _ _ e _ _ _ t _ _ n _ _ t

4 Circle the correct answer, a, b or c. (5 points)

1 ___ a secretary.
   a Her   b Your   **c** She's

2 What's ___ job?
   a his   b he's   c she

3 What's ___ name?
   a he's   b your   c she

4 Where's ___ from?
   a he   b I   c her

5 How old is ___ ?
   a you   b she   c he's?

6 ___ an artist.
   a I'm   b His   c Your

5 Write the sentences. (5 points)

1 He / singer.
   He's a singer.
2 Anna / police officer.
   _____
3 She / Polish.
   _____
4 Adam / electrician.
   _____
5 Her name / Helen.
   _____
6 She / from Russia.
   _____

6 Put the words in the correct order to make sentences. (5 points)

1 a / is / waiter. / He
   He is a waiter.
2 Kelly / actor. / isn't / Mr / an
   _____
3 not / engineer. / I / an / am
   _____
4 teacher / Mrs / your / Is / Thomas?
   _____
5 is / a / Tim / from / mechanic / Ireland.
   _____
6 from / You / not / France. / are
   _____

Total ____ /30

I know	Yes	No	?
• to be: am/'m not/am I?	☐	☐	☐
• to be: are/aren't/are you?	☐	☐	☐
• to be: is/isn't/is he?	☐	☐	☐
• my/your/his/her	☐	☐	☐
• I/you/he/she/it	☐	☐	☐
• a/an	☐	☐	☐

11

READING AND WRITING

A. His first name's Enrique and his surname's Morales. He isn't from the USA, he's from Puerto Rico. He's a singer, too.

B. She's American. She's from New York in the USA. She's a singer. Her first name's Alicia and her surname's Augello-Cook.

C. His first name's thomas and his surname is Mapother IV. he isn't a Singer, he's an Actor. he's from the usa.

D. florian Cloud de Bouinevialle Armstrong isn't american. she isn't French. she's from london, england. she's a Singer.

1 Look at the photos and read texts A–D. Match names 1–4 to the texts.

1 Tom Cruise — C
2 Ricky Martin ☐
3 Dido ☐
4 Alicia Keys ☐

2 Read the box and look at texts A and B. Tick (✓) the correct answers.

We use capital letters for:	
• countries (England)	✓
• nationalities (English)	☐
• jobs	☐
• names (Mary, London)	☐
• I (I am)	☐
• to start a sentence	☐

3 Correct texts C and D.

4 Write four or five sentences about a person (a friend/singer/actor). Use texts A–D to help you.

Penelope Cruz is from Spain. She …

PRONUNCIATION

/ɑː/ /æ/

1 **CD T9** Say the words. Then listen and repeat.

1 /ɑː/
/frɑːns/ France
/ˈɑːtɪst/ artist

2 /æ/
/bæg/ bag
/ˈkænədə/ Canada

2 **CD T10** Put the words from the box in the correct column. Then listen and check.

<u>aren't</u> Italian pardon Dan married
Martin Spanish mechanic afternoon
thanks

/ɑː/	/æ/
aren't	

3 Write sentences 1–4. Then tick (✓) the correct sentence, a or b.

1 /juː/ /ɑːnt/ /ən/ /ˈɑːtɪst/
   <u>You aren't an artist</u>.

2 /dæn/ /ɪz/ /ˈmærɪd/
   _____.

3 /dæn/ /ɪz/ /ə/ /mɪˈkænɪk/
   _____.

4 /ˈmɑːtɪn/ /ɪz/ /ən/ /ˈɑːtɪst/ /frəm/ /frɑːns/
   _____.

a Dan's an artist. ☐
b Martin's from France. ☐

SURVIVAL ENGLISH

Excuse me ...

1 **CD T11** Put the conversation in the correct order. Then listen and check.

a It's a bank. ☐
b Pardon? ☐
c Oh, a bank! Sorry, I don't know. ☐
d Excuse me. Where's HSBC? ☐ 1
e HSBC? I'm sorry, I'm from Germany. I don't understand. ☐
f HSBC. ☐

2 Complete the conversations. Circle a, b or c.

1 ___ Where's the bank, please?
   a Excuse me.
   b Pardon.
   c Good afternoon.

2 Thank you very much.
   a I'm sorry.
   b I don't understand.
   c You're welcome.

3 Are you Daniel Craig?
   a I don't know.
   b Pardon?
   c Excuse me.

GRAMMAR AND LISTENING

to be: is/isn't

1 Look at the photos and complete the sentences with *'s/isn't*.

1 Jack _isn't_ an engineer.
He _____ an actor.

2 Brigitte _____ Canadian.
She _____ French.

3 Miss Thomas _____ a doctor.
She _____ a teacher.

to be: is – questions and short answers

2 Write questions and short answers.

1 she / engineer?
Is she an engineer ?
Yes, she is . (+)
2 he / from Italy?
_____?
_____. (−)
3 Miss Thomas / your teacher?
_____?
_____. (−)
4 Jack / married?
_____?
_____. (+)
5 your name / Alice?
_____?
_____. (−)

3 Complete the questions.

1 _What's her name_ ? Her name's Tania.
2 _____ Turkey? No, he isn't. He's from Argentina.
3 How _____ she? She's nineteen.
4 Where _____ ? He's from Poland.
5 _____ Bart? No, it isn't. His name's Brian.
6 _____ his _____ ? He's an artist.

VOCABULARY

Spelling: the alphabet

1 **CD T8** Listen and write the answers.

1 What's your name?
It's _Sheila. S-h-e-i-l-a_ .
2 Are you German?
Yes, I'm from _____ .
3 Where's Rio de Janeiro?
It's in _____ .
4 Where's Peter from?
He's from _____ .
5 How old are you?
I'm _____ .
6 Is Maria Italian?
No, she's _____ .

2 **Puzzle** Complete the missing letters of the alphabet.

| a | | g | j | | p | | v | |

READING

1 **T5** Read the first part of the article. How many questions can you answer?

2 **T6** Read the second part of the article. Check your answers to Exercise 1.

FAMOUS PARENTS

1

Try our celebrity parent quiz – then check your answers in the article.

1 Brooklyn, Romeo and Cruz are brothers. Their father is David. Who's their mother?

2 Fifi Trixibelle, Peaches Honeyblossom and Pixie are sisters. Who's their father?

3 Apple's father is Chris. Who's her mother?

4 Sage and Seargeoh are brothers. Their sisters are Sophia, Sistine and Scarlet. Who's their father?

5 Who's Quinn's mother?

2

Celebrity children's names are different. David and Victoria Beckham's three children are Brooklyn, Romeo and Cruz. OK, Brooklyn and Romeo are unusual – Brooklyn is a district of New York and Romeo is a character from a Shakespeare play. But Cruz is a beautiful, traditional Spanish name. No problem? Hold on a minute. It's a girl's name and Cruz Beckham is a boy.

Sir Bob Geldof's three daughters are Fifi Trixibelle, Peaches Honeyblossom and Pixie. And Chris Martin (of Coldplay) and Gwyneth Paltrow's daughter's name is Apple. Is she a new friend for Peaches?

Sylvester Stallone's sons' names are Sage and Seargeoh. His daughters are Sophia, Sistine and Scarlet. How s-s-s-sweet.

Finally, it isn't strange that actress Patricia Quinn's son's name is Quinn. But Quinn is his first name and his surname. His full name is Quinn Quinn.

3 Read the article again and circle the correct answers.

1 Cruz is Romeo's
 a sister. b brother. c father.

2 Fifi Trixiebell is Bob's
 a daughter. b son. c mother.

3 Chris is Apple's
 a brother. b son. c father.

4 Sage is Sistine's
 a sister. b brother. c son.

5 Quinn is Patricia's
 a mother. b daughter. c son.

GRAMMAR

Possessive *s*

Singular nouns: add *'s*

*It's John**'s** book.   Sally's husband**'s** a doctor.*

Regular plural nouns: add *'*

*This is my parents**'** house.*

Irregular plural nouns:

*The children**'s** school is in Germany.*
*The women**'s** names are Olga and Petra.*
*The men**'s** T-shirts are from the USA.*

Mind the trap!

- *My brother**'s** friends* = one brother
  *My brothers**'** friend* = more than one brother
- We say *John and Sally's daughter*
  not ~~John's and Sally's daughter~~.

1 Look at the family tree. Complete the sentences.

Philip + Elizabeth

Charles   Anne

1 Philip is <u>Elizabeth's</u> husband.
2 Elizabeth is _____ wife.
3 Charles is _____ brother.
4 Anne is _____ sister.

2 Circle the possessive *s*.

1 John's Peter(s)brother.
2 John's wife's French.
3 Annie's John's wife.
4 Annie's dad's a doctor.
5 Sophie's Annie's mum.
6 John's mum's Helen.
7 Helen's husband's Mike.
8 Michel's Annie's brother.

3 Match the pictures with the sentences.

1 This is a picture of my sister's sons. ☐
2 This is a picture of my sisters' sons. ☐

LISTENING AND SPEAKING

1 **T2** Listen to the conversation and write the phone numbers.

Name: <u>Nick Green</u>
Home: _____
Work: _____
Mobile: _____

2 **T3** Listen to the telephone conversation and circle what the people say.

Receptionist	World Music. ¹(Good morning)/ Good afternoon.
Anne	Hello. Is Simon Parke there?
Receptionist	² *Hold on,* / *Hang on a minute,* please.
Simon	Hello.
Anne	³ *Hello* / *Hi* Simon. ⁴ *This is Anne.* / *Anne here.* / *It's Anne.*
Simon	Hi Anne. How are you?
Anne	⁵ *Very well,* / *Fine,* / *Not bad,* thank you. And you?
Simon	I'm OK.
Anne	Simon, where's John this week?
Simon	He's in Tokyo.
Anne	Oh, of course. Thanks. See you ⁶ *soon,* / *later,* / *tomorrow,* then.
Simon	See you. ⁷ *Bye.* / *Bye Bye.* / *Goodbye.* Take care.
Anne	Bye.

3 **T4** Put the conversation in the correct order. Then listen and check.

a Bye. Take care. ☐
b Good morning. World Music. ☐
c Hang on a minute. It's 07789 233 066. ☐1☐
d Hello Marlene. This is Tom. How are you? ☐
e Hello. This is Marlene Katz. Is Patty Vincennes there? ☐
f Hi Tom. I'm fine, thank you. And you? ☐
g No problem. What's her mobile number? ☐
h Thanks very much. Bye, Tom. ☐
i Very well, thanks. But Patty isn't here today. She's in London. ☐

02 Jobs

GRAMMAR AND VOCABULARY

he/she, his/her

1 Complete the conversations.

1 A What's <u>his</u> name?
  B His name's <u>Neil</u>.
  A Where's <u>he</u> from?
  B He's from <u>Ireland</u>.

2 A What's _____ name?
  B Her name's _____ .
  A Where's _____ from?
  B She's from _____ .

3 A _____ name?
  B His name's _____ .
  A _____ from?
  B He's from _____ .

4 A What's _____ name?
  B Her _____ .
  A _____ from?
  B She's _____ .

5 A _____ name?
  B _____ name's _____ .
  A _____ from?
  B _____ from _____ .

6 A _____ ?
  B _____ .
  A _____ ?
  B _____ .

Vocabulary: jobs

2 Write the jobs.

1 c t a y r s e e r   _secretary_
2 c o r a t   _____
3 t r s i t e o e p i n c   _____
4 g s r e i n   _____
5 n e i e g n r e   _____

3 Write the jobs in the boxes.

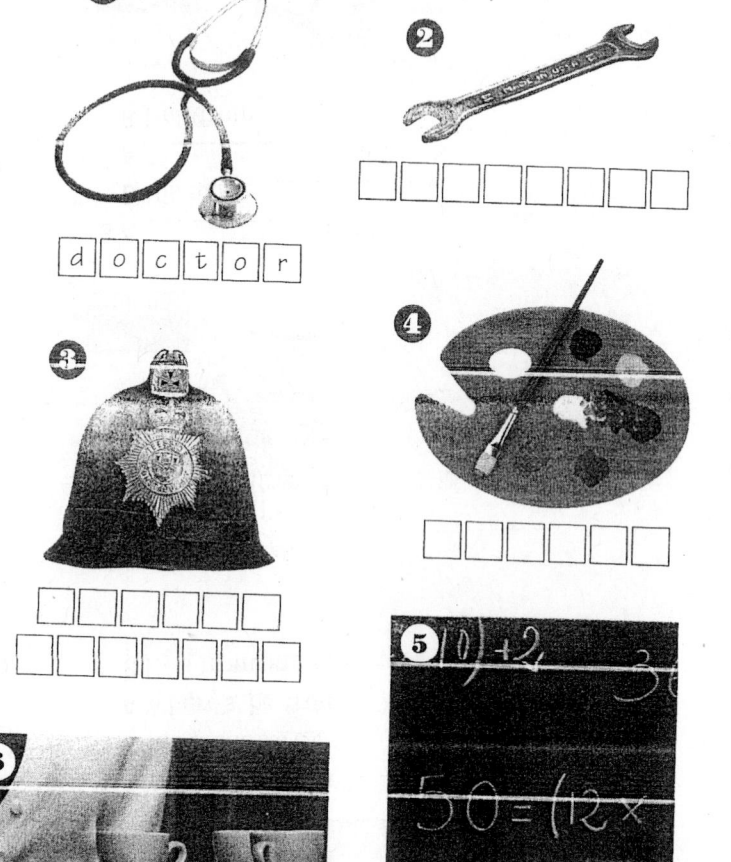

① | d | o | c | t | o | r |

② □□□□□□□

③ □□□□□ □□□□□□

④ □□□□□□

⑤ □□□□□□□

⑥ □□□□□

a/an

4 Write *a* or *an* in the correct place.

1 His name's Andy. He's ⟨a⟩ mechanic.

2 I'm from Poland. I'm engineer.

3 Marie's receptionist. She's from France.

4 Are you secretary?

5 Tom's actor from London.

6 Her name's Jill and she's artist.

to be: *is*/*'s*

5 Write the sentences with *'s*.

1 Her name Katie.
   Her name's Katie.
2 Katie from London.

   _____

3 She a receptionist.

   _____

4 His name Bülent.

   _____

5 He an engineer.

   _____

6 Bülent Turkish.

   _____

he/she is, you are, your/his/her

6 Tick (✓) the correct sentence.

1 a She's a secretary.   ✓
  b She are a secretary.   □

2 a What's he's job?   □
  b What's his job?   □

3 a What's your name?   □
  b What's you're name.   □

4 a Where are you from?   □
  b Where she is from?   □

5 a How old is you?   □
  b How old is she?   □

6 a His job is an artist.   □
  b He's an artist.   □

7 Answer the questions about Mike Brown.

Jobs 4U

NAME:	Mike Brown
JOB:	Engineer
COUNTRY:	Canada
AGE:	22

1 What's his name?
   His name's Mike Brown.
2 What's his job?

   _____

3 Where is he from?

   _____

4 How old is he?

   _____

5 Read and complete the Student Visa form.

Hi. I'm Lisa Rossi. I'm from Rome. I'm 19 and I'm not married.

UK visas

Student Visa
1 Surname: <u>Rossi</u>
2 First name: _____
3 Age: _____
4 Married ☐   Single ☐
5 Country: _____
6 Address: <u>Piazza Danti, 7a,</u>
<u>001856</u>
_____

6 Write the nationalities.

1 Australia — <u>Australian</u>
2 China — _____
3 England — _____
4 France — _____
5 Hungary — _____
6 Japan — _____
7 Poland — _____
8 Russia — _____
9 the USA — _____

7 Complete the texts with *in*, *at* or *on*.

'This is a great photo. It's me with my sisters. We're ¹<u>in</u> the garden ²____ home. I'm ³____ the middle, Kate's ⁴____ the left and Nicola's ⁵____ the right. Our brother John isn't ⁶____ the photo. He's ⁷____ university ⁸____ Edinburgh.

Hello. Is that Jane? Hi Jane. It's me. I'm ⁹____ Amsterdam. Yes. Amsterdam. I'm ¹⁰____ a café. Yes. A café. I'm ¹¹____ holiday. It's great here. Where are you? You're ¹²____ school? Ha ha. Sorry!

WRITING

1 Add capital letters and apostrophes to the email.

From: nuria@abc.com
To: annie.benson@yes.com
Subject: HI!

hi annie,

how are you? im in prague with jane and her family. their house is beautiful – its near the university. janes dads english but her mums czech. shes a teacher and hes a doctor. theyre great but her brothers stupid.

this is a photo of jane and me. were on charles bridge.

im the beautiful one!

jane sends her love.

see you soon,

nuria

xxx

WORD LIST

- address
- age
- at home/school/ a barbecue/a party
- aunt
- Australia
- (at a) barbecue
- beautiful
- big
- birthday
- boy
- boyfriend
- Brazil
- brother
- child (pl children)
- China
- Chinese
- city
- class
- country
- cousin
- daughter
- day
- doctor
- Egypt
- Egyptian
- England
- English
- family
- family tree
- father/dad
- favourite
- first name
- France
- French
- friend
- friendly
- German
- Germany
- girl
- grandchildren
- grandfather
- grandmother
- grandparents
- grandson
- great
- house
- Hungarian
- Hungary
- husband
- in a classroom/garden/ photo/café
- in the middle
- Italian
- Italy
- Japan
- Japanese
- job
- language school
- little
- local
- man (pl men)
- married
- month
- mother/mum
- name
- nephew
- next to
- niece
- on holiday
- on my left/right
- parents
- person (pl people)
- phone number
- Poland
- Polish
- Russia
- Russian
- single
- sister
- son
- Spain
- Spanish
- stepfather
- stepmother
- student
- surname
- teacher
- teenager
- the USA
- T-shirt
- Turkey
- Turkish
- uncle
- university
- very
- week
- what
- where
- who
- wife
- woman (pl women)
- young

VOCABULARY

1 Complete the crossword with family words.

Across 1: GRANDCHILDREN

ACROSS ▶
1 Your daughter's children are your ... (13)
3 Your grandparent's children are your ... (7)
8 Your father's brother's daughter is your ... (6)
9 Your father's grandchildren are your ... (8)
10 Your father's mother is your ... (11)

DOWN ▼
1 Your mother's father is your ... (11)
2 Your brother's son is your ... (6)
4 Your sister's daughter is your ... (5)
5 Your mother's brother is your ... (5)
6 Your father's son is your ... (7)
7 Your mother's daughter is your ... (6)
11 Your father's sister is your ... (4)

2 Match the opposites.

1 girlfriend — c
2 married
3 mum
4 wife
5 daughter

a single
b son
c boyfriend
d dad
e husband

3 Find the plurals in the Word list.

1 man — men
2 woman _____
3 child _____
4 person _____

4 Circle the 'odd one out'.

1 doctor / teacher / (teenager) / student
2 at home / at university / at school / at half past six
3 on the right / on holiday / on the left / in the middle
4 women / men / children / family
5 in a photo / in London / in a classroom / in a café

10

Making contact

GRAMMAR

to be affirmative and negative

	Affirmative	Negative
I	am ('m) on holiday.	am not ('m not) at home.
We/You/They	are ('re) Italian.	are not (aren't) American.
He/She/It	is ('s) in London.	is not (isn't) in Madrid.

Mind the trap!
We say *She's 21.* not *She has 21.*

Possessive adjectives

Subject pronouns	Possessive adjectives
I	my
you	your
she	her
he	his
it	its
we	our
you	your
they	their

1 Complete the sentences with the correct form of the verb *to be*: affirmative (+) or negative (−).

1 Tom **is** from Paris. (+)
2 We _____ good friends. (−)
3 I _____ an English student. (+)
4 Kevin and Ali _____ on holiday. (+)
5 Anna _____ my best friend. (+)
6 I _____ a doctor. (−)
7 Steve _____ 21. (+)
8 Jenny _____ at school today. (−)

2 Write the sentences.

1 We / not in Spain / France
   We aren't in Spain. We're in France.
2 Beyoncé Knowles / not British / American
   _____
3 David Beckham / not from Manchester / London
   _____
4 Penelope Cruz and Antonio Banderas / not English / Spanish
   _____
5 Pizza / not from France / Italy
   _____
6 I / not a teacher / student
   _____

3 Circle the correct words.

1 John is *I /* **my** *father's best friend.
2 *He / His* is from New York.
3 *He / His* is a doctor.
4 *He / His / Her* wife is a teacher.
5 *She / Her / His* is Spanish.
6 *She / Her / His* parents are from the north of Spain.
7 *They / They're / Their* house is in Burgos.
8 *They / They're / Their* are teachers, too.

4 Complete the text with possessive adjectives.

'This is a photo of ¹**my** friend, Jenny. She's from England, but ² _____ parents are Russian. This is ³ _____ house in Brighton. It's very big! She's with ⁴ _____ boyfriend. ⁵ _____ name's Dale.

This is me with ⁶ _____ mum and dad. We're on holiday. This is ⁷ _____ house in Spain.

This is my brother and ⁸ _____ girlfriend in Paris. ⁹ _____ dad's an English teacher.

Now you show me ¹⁰ _____ photos.'

6

GRAMMAR

to be questions

Yes/No questions			Short answers
Am	I		Yes, I am / No, I'm not.
Are	we / you / they	Italian?	Yes, he/she/it is. / No, he/she/it isn't.
Is	he / she / it		Yes, we/you/they are. / No, we/you/they aren't.

Mind the trap!
- Saying just *yes* or *no* can be impolite. Say, eg *Yes, I am.* or *No, I'm not.*
- We say *Yes, I am.* not *Yes, I'm.*

Wh- questions
What's your name?
Where are you from?
How old are your parents?
Who's your teacher?

---

1 Write Yes/No questions.

1 You're married.
   <u>Are you married?</u>
2 He's Russian.
   _____
3 She's on holiday.
   _____
4 They're in Rome.
   _____
5 He's a teacher.
   _____
6 You're 21.
   _____

2 Write the Wh- questions for these answers.

1 <u>Where are you from?</u>
   I'm from Madrid.
2 _____
   My name's Alicia.
3 _____
   I'm 17.
4 _____
   My phone number is 91 329 778.
5 _____
   My best friend's Paloma.
6 _____
   She's from Barcelona.

3 Match the answers with the questions.

1 Is Brad Pitt English?
2 Is Jim Carrey from the USA?
3 Is Penelope Cruz Spanish?
4 Is New York the capital of the USA?
5 Are Beijing and Shanghai in China?
6 Is Nicole Kidman from France?
7 Is Michael Schumacher German?
8 Is Ottawa the capital of Canada?

1 b

a No, it isn't. It's Washington DC.
b ~~No, he isn't. He's American.~~
c No, she isn't. She's Australian.
d No, he isn't. He's from Canada.
e Yes, he is.
f Yes, she is.
g Yes, they are.
h Yes, it is.

4 Write answers that are true for you.

1 Are you from Moscow?
   _____
2 Is your name Ben?
   _____
3 Are you single?
   _____
4 Are you on holiday?
   _____
5 Are you 16?
   _____